ORIGINS OF FORM

ORIGINS OF FORM

The Shape of Natural and Man-made Things

CHRISTOPHER WILLIAMS

Architectural Book Publishing Company

TAYLOR TRADE PUBLISHING

Lanham • New York • Boulder • Toronto • Plymouth, UK

This book is for Cornelia Britenbach.

My gratitude to the Graham Foundation for Advanced Studies in the Fine Arts, for their generous help.

Architectural Book Publishing Company

Published by Taylor Trade Publishing
An imprint of The Rowman & Littlefield Publishing Group, Inc.
4501 Forbes Boulevard, Suite 200, Lanham, Maryland 20706
www.rowman.com

10 Thornbury Road, Plymouth PL6 7PP, United Kingdom

Distributed by National Book Network

The original edition of this book was previously catalogued by the Library of Congress. Catalog Card Number: 80-39594.

ISBN 978-1-57979-808-3 (pbk. : alk. paper)

∞™ The paper used in this publication meets the minimum requirements of American National Standard for Information Sciences—Permanence of Paper for Printed Library Materials, ANSI/NISO Z39.48-1992.

Printed in the United States of America

CONTENTS

Cross-functionalism—for one cause, but against another
Trans-functionalism—to unite opposing causes
Function, time and change—all things go through the following process:
    Equilibrium—remaining static within a time-frame
    Dynamic—the inevitable change
    Creative—the old gives rise to the new
Form, function and economy, why some forms endure

PREFACE TO THE NEW EDITION

The simplest of truths and the greatest inspirations lie just beyond our doors: out over the fence and into the woods, even in the vacant lot down the street. It is here that there is a source of insight for the things we create.

The great master builders, artists, designers, and inventors of our times have not been directed by current trends or styles but by the vast unifying principles of the natural world around us.

This whole book is intended as a preface, an introduction to awareness of the natural reasoning behind the shapes things take. All of the material world, the tree, the mountain, and the chair we sit upon, are formed from a scant one hundred elements like iron, bismuth, gold, lithium, and tungsten. These elements are assembled and reassembled into a near infinity of basic matter, like the wood of the tree, which makes our chair. The raw material is then reshaped by our hands into forms that suit our needs. As this shaping takes place, there is also a near infinity of influences on these developing forms, directing their outcomes. Just as the principles of the English language direct the twenty-six letters of our alphabet into meaningful words, sentences, and thoughts, the laws of nature direct these elements of our physical world into meaningful forms. A grasp of the way things best fit together, be it a language or an object, is essential.

As we become evermore insular in our "built environment," the more important becomes our need to see beyond our barriers and to remember our teacher and inspiration.

Christopher Williams
Big Sur, California   2012

INTRODUCTION

"It does not appear fitted for any mode of life," said the third wise man. . . . "It is not swift of foot, it cannot climb trees, it cannot dig holes in the earth. It has no means of supporting its own life, or escaping from its enemies."

"If it is a living animal," said the schoolmaster, "then we must acknowledge that nature sometimes makes a mistake.". . .

"Yes . . . it is a freak of nature," said they all and bowed themselves out of the room.

—Upon attempting to identify the diminutive Gulliver, from *Gulliver's Travels* by Jonathan Swift

Possibly life started on this planet in a warm saline pool by the shores of a cooling ocean somewhere between three and five billion years ago. It might have happened that somewhere in this indistinctive crevice of water the molecularly correct amounts of carbon, hydrogen, nitrogen, and oxygen were present and correctly juxtaposed during an Archeozoic thunderstorm. The charged elements united and an amino acid was formed. This situation may have been repeated countlessly over vast stretches of time in many environments, with failures and successes only to result in later failures. Eventually some amino acids formed proteins which gave rise to an algae, probably the first plants. The algae became the food for the freshly formed single-celled protozoa, the first true animals.

Modifications and limitations altered form and structure as millions of years slipped by; one species branched and divided, and change compounded change. The pyramid descended from its apex and finally the only commonality that remained was the essence of life and the link of heredity all the way back to that primary existence. The first gives rise to the second, which gives rise to the third; from the simple comes the complex. Each owes its life and own aspects to its predecessor, but after the inheritance is received and before it is passed on, the slightest change is made, and whole new families start en route.

The multiplying families and species helped one another but also competed with each other. The most successful discovered specialized environments to occupy and methods to employ in their lives. Specialization became the mode of survival. Some life forms found a way of living in the deep sea, or by migrating through host organisms, or by swimming fast, or digging deep, or existing in the desert, or puffing themselves up to escape their enemies.

Only during the most recent moments of biological history the hominid lineage began to take form; from the start something was very different.

The pre-toolmaking humanoids may have had little to distinguish them visually from their predecessors, but the changes were taking place inside. The central nervous system was becoming finely developed, the brain capacity expanded, the eyes became able to focus on a fixed point for extended periods of time, the posture became erect, which enabled this pre-man to run and keep cool away from the ground, and sometimes even outrun its prey. The more erect posture threw the head back for balance and turned the eyes out to a wide field of vision, which was needed when early man moved out of the forest into the open plain where life was more dangerous.

This new creature was not the swiftest runner, swimmer, or digger of holes. It could no longer swing from the trees so surely, it had underdeveloped slashing and grinding teeth, and it may not have been the best hunter nor fruit gatherer, but it was the only animal that could do all of these things, if only adequately. This new animal had no specialization and no special environment. The first generalist had been born.

It has been said that the human hand, even with its opposing thumb, is not specialized. Writes Kenneth Oakley, an anthropologist, "Regarded anatomically the prehensile hand of the less specialized monkeys would be capable of making tools if directed by an adequate brain; in many ways our own hands are more primitive than those of the anthropoid apes, our closest living relatives. In fact the pentadactyl, or five-fingered hand, of man is so generalized that one would have to seek among the first mammals, or even go back to the reptiles from which they were derived, to find such primitive simplicity."

Our hands are the tools of a generalist, perhaps not the best at picking fleas or cracking shells, grasping branches, treading water, or even building a house or operating a keyboard. However, as with our bodies, these hands can do all of these things, if only adequately well.

Though crude they may be, these five-fingered hands are directed by an acutely sensitive central nervous system and a creative and purposeful brain, and so they can become makers of tools, and it is the tools they make that can gain the specialization the hand cannot and cause humans to be experts and specialists at almost anything.

We fly higher, dig deeper, move faster, and build larger than anything that has ever inhabited the earth for these three billion years. Humans can, but also humans must. Almost every other creature of the earth has a special place and a specific purpose in that place with which they have evolved. Mankind began in the savannahs but rapidly spread throughout the rest of the world. Few places are our natural home, so we must alter them to accommodate our needs to make them habitable for us.

Though alien to many aspects of the biological network, the things that people build, the way they are formed, the materials that are employed, the laws that control the size and structure, are not any different from those that operate through the natural world. The things that we build have an appearance that is uniquely human, and so it should be, but the methodology behind the form is planetary.

This book is a call to anyone who is interested in the world they inhabit to break away from assumptions and indifference to our built environment, the environment that is so much a part of our lives. These following pages attempt to encourage the reader to become more aware by looking about and understanding the complexities of the natural world, and thus seeing what is possible and what is not, what should be built and what should not. This book is a call to see the limits of size, the vernacular of a material, how elements relate, and how history, function, and structure control, and if an object should be made otherwise.

The notions and facts here were gathered from many sources: the areas of mechanics, structure, and materials; geology, biology, anthropology, paleobiology, morphology; and others. These are standard facts to naturalists, but they should also be familiar references to anyone who desires a knowledge and understanding of the world around us.

We began as generalists and for two million years, human activities have become more pervasive and more generalized. But as society has become more generalized, individuals have become more specialized and insular, especially in recent years.

A new era is at hand, an era that will call for broad knowledge and deep perceptions. A new generation of people need to arise with an overview to understand and guide human activity through this critical portion of time. We need to go back to our origins as generalists and reestablish our understandings of the natural world.

1 FORM AND MATTER

Propelled by the helter-skelter cascading of gaseous compounds, mixtures, molecules and free atoms, a single hydrogen atom is thrown apart from the vent of a bubbling charging car battery in the turbulent engine compartment of a speeding car. With a rush of wind the hydrogen atom is carried free into the air of the countryside beside the interstate highway. The atom has just been released from a compound of hydrochloric acid in the car battery, a short involvement of only two years total since its last free state. The car quickly disappears and the last circle of wind throws the atom high above the pasture where it drifts westward twenty feet from the ground. Within seconds two other atoms ricochet simultaneously into the hydrogen atom and instantaneously form a molecule. The atom's free state is quickly over. One of the new associates is another hydrogen atom, the other oxygen. The new unit is a water molecule. The brand-new molecule zig-zags upward in a late afternoon thermal current.

The season is dry; the air contains few water particles and molecules. But despite the relative isolation, other molecules of water bounce about on the upward float; when they pass within a short range of each other they immediately unite. Molecules join molecules and the new grouping becomes a distinguishable speck of water, sedately drifting a thousand feet above a field of alfalfa. The sun sets, the air cools, the moisture gathers and the speck of water grows so large with the new additions that it can no longer stay aloft; it falls.

In the early morning of the next day a sphere of dew containing the hydrogen atom rests on an alfalfa leaf. More water particles soon join it, and the droplet rolls into the earth. The day heats up and most of the moisture near the surface of the pasture breaks down into water vapor again and lifts off. Our hydrogen atom, though, is contained in a molecule that drops farther into the soil. There it resides for three days until a searching root hair from a nearby alfalfa plant pushes through the air pockets between the soil specks. The root tip builds cell upon cell in linear pulses; each cell brings the tip about a ten thousandth of an inch closer. The root hair makes contact with the moisture-bearing soil and rapidly imbibes the molecule.

For the next five hours the hydrogen atom is shuffled into and out of complex and simple compounds and moved through two and one half meters of sap conduction tubes. Finally it rests in a molecule with six carbon atoms, six oxygen atoms, and eleven other hydrogen atoms in a viscous liquid compound called glucose. Our atom occupies a molecule at the backmost edge of the third leaf from the top of a large but unhealthy alfalfa plant near the southernmost corner of the field.

July moves into August and August into September. The alfalfa is harvested, dried, bundled, and lofted in the barn. The alfalfa leaf is eaten by a cow in February. During the hours after being eaten, the hydrogen atom is liberated and reabsorbed in a volley of chemical processes and movements called digestion, absorption, circulation, distribution, and utilization. By that midnight, the atom is firmly lodged in a compound in the wall of a newly formed hair follicle deep inside the hide covering the cow's flanks. The hair grows over the winter and drops out in the mud of the spring pasture. Sun, warmth, moisture, and bacteria break the hair down again in decay and an eddy of wind picks up the bouncing liberated hydrogen atom above the barnyard.

These interludes are short with the haste of organic life. Stone, however, can trap an atom for billions of years. The atom's travel then comes about only through the changing conditions of the earth's surface. The possibility of an atom's early release thousands of feet beneath the earth's surface is very slight.

Atoms are the smallest group that defines material substance. Within the composition of the atom the characteristics of materials are determined. The atom is the block for building the elements. Atoms are very sound units, able to remain intact through almost any onslaught of forces that they encounter: heat, chemical reaction, and electrical charge. Most atoms are stable enough to last through innumerable years. Some of the time is spent alone as independent unassociated atoms adrift in space. Some atoms spend more time independently than others for they have fewer compatible associates, other atoms with which they would readily join. Some quick joiners like carbon and oxygen may pass through a nearly infinite procession of materials in a spiralling cycle of growth and decay and growth again. The materials are formed and proceed through their limited existence to eventual dispersement and destruction, and the atoms go round and round. (1)

Material definition stops at the atom but matter can be traced on down into ever smaller composites. When followed into inner space the sub-atomic specks of matter (electrons, protons, and an increasing number of newly discovered particles) continue to be found to be divided and subdivided into what may be an infinite process of dimunition. Matter may be impossible to identify from a point of origin. There may be no coherent particle upon which all that we know as substance rests. The space between the disappearing matter, though, is totally coherent, a continuum from the infinitely small in a consistent

flow into and beyond the universe. Ultimately space may be more a reality than matter, matter may be negative, accumulations of holes adrift and in suspension in the solidarity of space.

We must, though, operate within our own range of acceptance. We know that matter is divided into three states and within our own time span our perceptions are reality. The three great divisions of matter are: liquids, solids, and gases. Perhaps the best way to perceive the three states is as a blend and to see matter from the inside and thus regard it in time and space.

At temperature above 3,000 degrees C. iron becomes vaporous. The molecules of iron are so charged with thermal energy that they cascade through space and would dissipate if not contained. Iron in this gaseous state contains so much space that it is difficult if not impossible to see. It weighs in the milligrams per cubic foot, has no form other than that of its container, and its volume is impossible to determine, for it is infinitely expandable. When cooled below 3,000 degrees C., iron vapor will precipitate and condense, reducing the space between its molecules as they become less active and fall in closer on one another. From about 3,000 to 1,500 degrees C., iron is in a liquid state. The volume is greatly reduced for a given quantity of matter, and this more gentle molecular activity results in a coherent liquid mass. At about 1,500 degrees C. the iron begins to crystallize. As molecular activity continues to decrease, space continues to shrink between the molecules; the crystalline latticework forms and the material is said to be a solid. The molecules, though

1-1 All materials exist in one of the three states of matter. Temperature and pressure regulate their disposition at any given time. Many substances are capable of passing from a gas to a liquid to a solid within a few degrees of temperature change. At normal atmospheric pressures water is gaseous or vaporous at about 100° C. (212° F.), liquid between 100° C. and 0° C. (32° F.) and solid below that temperature. Not many substances can change so dramatically with such little temperature change. Other materials may ignite at room temperature like phosphorus; still other substances we have come to regard as liquid, like mercury, are in actuality a melted metal, only solidifying at minus 38° C.

1-2 Solid unheated iron that has been squeezed under very high pressure flows like a semi-liquid. This drawing was made from a photograph of a polished section of iron which was deformed between two dies, then etched with a diluted solution of hydrochloric acid to reveal the fibrous bands of iron as they push one another toward the opening in the die, the point of least resistance. Iron is not homogeneous, but consists of many compounds and impurities which the pressure and flow form into stratifications called "Luders" bands.

12

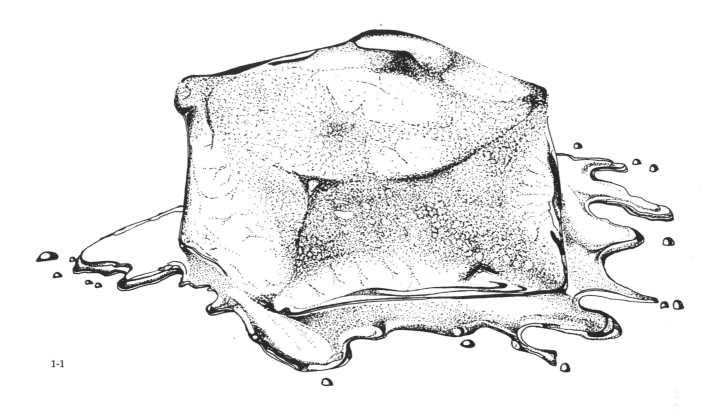

1-1

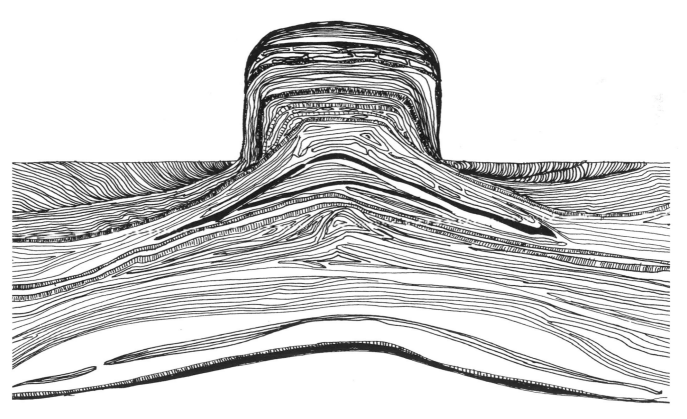

1-2

held relatively firmly within their geometric interlocking, still vibrate with excitement with the reminiscence of their thermal energy. In theory, if heat continues to be drawn from the material, more space is eliminated from between the molecules as molecular activity slows to a point of no movement at absolute zero, perhaps an impossible state to reach.

Grasping the unity between these three states is often more revealing than defining their differences. The world as we know it is a whole and all its parts respond to the same earthly laws; all substance about us has the same physiochemical basis; all particles of matter are moulded by the same physical laws. The structural unity is time.

Given enough time all matter is fluid. Geology, the study of time and matter, sees the rigid structure of the earth's surface heaving, shrinking, folding, and sliding like a frantic bedsheet in the wind. The geologist's view is from the billion year point, past which the panorama of the land forms flash. The granite mountain range is a momentary wrinkle not there yesterday and gone tomorrow. Deep within the earth's crust round pebbles turned under, after a millenium above ground, by the thrust of subterranean plates become bound in solidifying clay. The round pebbles of solid crystalline rock flow under vast pressures into ellipses and then discs as billions of years squash them into different compositions and shapes in the metamorphic environment.

The flow of solid material can also be described in hundreds of years. Glaciers of compacted ice flow like rivers, expressing their hundred-year minutes. Old church windows slowly ooze down to their bottom sides where the colored glass gathers over the centuries. The grain in a tree's growth is chronicled in tens of years as it flows around knots and hollows as the tree moves its structure to follow its shape. (2)

As they flow from one form to another, different materials often respond in the same way when subjected to a similar action. A block of steel clamped beneath the cutting tool of a milling machine will reflect familiar patterns as the cutting arm moves back and forth over the surface of the block. Each cut takes a shave of steel that folds back like the wave of soil from the leading edge of a plow and the bow wake from a boat moving through the water. If time were disregarded, the materials of the earth's surface could be seen to cascade, flow, creep and ooze from a position of resistance to gravity into a position of acquiescence. Their speed of movement is determined by their resistance to the pull of gravity, or their relative solidity.

The result of all the vast geological powers in action is movement of the materials of the earth's outer crust to a position either up or down. The up movement is usually violent and massive. Sheets of earth thousands of feet thick fold and buckle into mountain ranges, like a shifting, breaking ice field. Pockets of liquid rock burst into sight and harden into conical volcanoes and islands. The action is quickly over and the results are impressive. The down movement and the leveling process, though, are always the final expression. They are seldom exciting and often scarcely detectable in their slowness. Water cloudy with a suspension of clay moves in trickles and lazy currents on great rivers to places hundreds of miles away to deposit the bits and specks of debris only a few feet lower than their points of origin. Sand, pebbles, and boulders roll along the bottom of river beds and slide down the sides of valleys. A ragged colluvium canyonside spread with sand, clay and rubble rock of all sizes imperceptibly creeps down the slope maybe no more than six inches a year. An ice age granite monolithic boulder dropped in a small bottomland plane by retreating ice sinks one half foot in three thousand years.

If the inner discontent of the earth were to be satisfied and the mountains stop their building, the wind and rain, the ice and sun, the plants and animals would, with slow but deliberate industry, wear all the high peaks, the plateaus and high pastures into the low places: the ocean trenches; sea

1-3 The machining of steel is dependent upon the ability of the material to flow. Pictured here is the leading edge of a cutting tool slicing five-thousandths of an inch from the surface of the steel workpiece. At the leading point of the cutting tool the cut material is separated and forced to flow up to form the spiralling chip. In clean smooth cutting it is essential that the chip clears the cutting zone to reduce friction, stress, and heat. At times when the tool is at an improper angle or dull, the tool "loads," which is the piling up of the cut material in front of the cutting edge. This action inhibits cutting and what is known as "smearing" results, a tearing roughly at the surface of the work.

1-4 To the left are crystals of sugar ($C_{12}H_{22}O_{11}$) and to the right is a single pigment cell of frog skin. In some ways both are typical of the categories they represent, mineral and organic. The sugar crystals begin their growth at a single point and build out in a radial direction. The individual crystals add layer upon layer to build their substances. The forms are of straight line and sharp angle. In the case of the frog cell, however, all the growth takes place within the boundaries of the cell wall, the growth pattern is more random, the form is rounded with curved lines. Sharp angles and straight lines are seldom seen in organic forms.

1-3

1-4

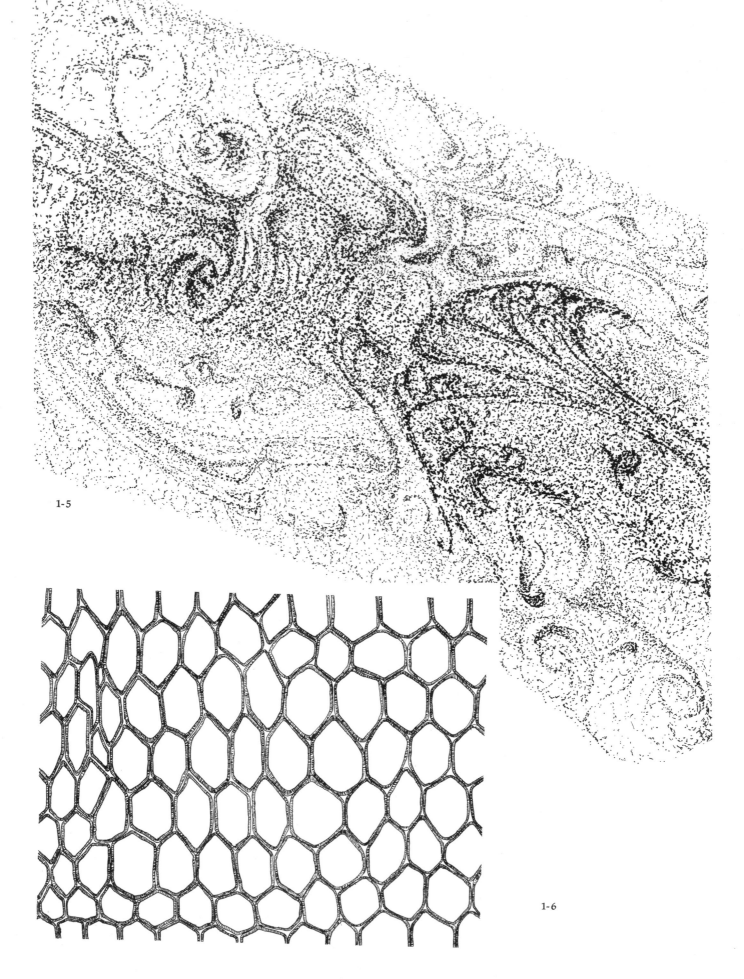

1-5

1-6

floors, and river valleys. Eventually there would be no high and no low; all would be equal and level. (3)

These processes, the taking apart and diminishing and the building and putting together, help cause the evolution of form into its vast variations. The first division of form control under the criteria of material comes from the influences of addition and those of subtraction. The second branching is between organic and chemical, and each goes through this growth and decline stage which affects its form in distinct and different ways.

The expanding organic form is usually a smooth rounded surface, with one edge flowing into another. The organic form is developed from the inside, as a balloon growing larger with compressed air. The adding of new material occurs within the organism: inside the tree's bark, leaf's surface, and human skin. The organic surface is pushed out in its attempt to contain the expanding substance bumping out from inside. A fresh green pea first out of the pod has a tight translucence to its polished surface. Growth compresses organic material into containers like feathers stuffed into a pillow. The inside is in compression, but the outside is in tension, and it is this stretch of the surface that is the key to the forms of organic origin.

To reconstruct the logic in the building process of the organic form it is necessary to digress temporarily to the explanation of the phenomenon called surface tension: an insect will drift upon the surface of a still

1-5 If the wall of a soap and water bubble could be sliced to reveal its cross-section it would look something like this. Because of a very unstable situation the membrane is in a state of frantic activity as an equalization is underway. Bodies of denser compounds swirl along the membrane center, convection currents from heat differences eddy through, water containing less soap spreads and air moves about the outside of the bubble, pushing particles before it on the bubble's surface. The center of the membrane is denser than the rest and so moves as a separate layer. Surface tension holds the whole system intact. the molecules on the inside attract the surface molecules which causes them to move inward. This constant movement of surface molecules to the interior causes a shrinkage, squeezing the bubble membrane thinner, effecting a surface tension. All this activity continues until one portion grows too thin, and the bubble bursts.

1-6 This drawing represents a rather typical situation of unspecialized cell wall structure. The walls are formed under a very strict set of physical conditions. Surface tension is one such phenomenon. Organic material is generally in a liquid state during the formation process. The energy from one surface attempts to transfer to the next and so equalizes. The result is a tendency for the cell wall to form an equalangular three-way intersection, resulting in the six-sided figure and the hexagonal pattern. With more specialized cells, like nerve or muscle cells, the function dominates the form. See chapter seven for more explanation.

lake with its legs, wings, and antennae denting pockets and hollows into the water's surface without becoming damp, for there is an invisible "skin" between the insect and the body of water beneath. This same skin makes it possible for water skeeters and other insects to skate and run upon the water's surface. Droplets of dew will stand on grass leaves and rain drops on a freshly waxed automobile by the same mechanism. The extreme outside edge of any liquid is in constant state of energy transfer. The molecules on the surface are attracted by those just beneath, and so are continually attempting to move from the outside to the interior.

The apparently placid surface of a soap bubble is actually in a state of frantic activity as the molecules dash madly between the three layers that comprise the thickness of the bubble: the inside surface, the center, and the outside surface. The two surfaces are in surface tension. The movement from the outer surface causes a continual surface shrinkage to take place, in effect tightening "skin" across and around the liquid. If the liquid is a raindrop, surface tension attempts to make that drop as spherical as possible as the outside shrinks.

Over a large body of water, surface tension exerts an insignificant effect, for gravity acting on the sheer volume overwhelms this molecular action. As the volume of liquid decreases, the proportional force of surface tension increases. Though small things will be supported on the surface tension of a large mass of water, the mass is not contained by it. Small raindrops are more spherical than large ones, and dewdrops are rounder still. The strength of surface tension increases dramatically in minute sizes and becomes a force equal to many atmospheres of pressure at sizes little larger than the molecules themselves.

The relationship of this molecular action to organic form is immediate and direct. Organic material has an extremely high percentage of its volume in water. When cell walls are formed they are in a viscous liquid state. The organic cell is small and the cell wall smaller still. Because of these minute sizes, cell formation is greatly influenced by surface tension. Surface tension would have only an insignificant effect upon a form as large as human being or a cow, but it has an overwhelming effect upon their cells, which in turn influence the form of the entire organism, and so the forms of animals and plants are controlled by surface tension acting upon their cells.

17

The kind of control surface tension exerts upon cell formation is this: when water is observed inside a glass container it can be noted that the outside perimeter of the water turns up at the edges to meet the surface of the glass, or when two bubbles intersect, their points of intersection blend into each other. Surface tension is an energy that is always seeking an equalization. It attempts to blend forms together and distribute the energy as evenly as possible; there is never a sharp corner found in liquid formation. When cells are formed, they are well blended into each other; each intersection is rounded at the corners as the forces of surface tension on each wall balance themselves, and so affect the cell wall form and in turn the cell and organic tissue.

We will be examining some other implications of surface tension in Chapter Seven, Teleology.

In contrast, the forms of mineral growth are angular with flat faces and sharp edges. Mineral growth is on the outside. Like a mason laying brick upon brick the mineral wall is erected in flat layers with sharp corners. All the activity is exterior; nothing happens on the inside after the substance is set in place. This type of angular growth can be seen from the smallest crystals of a few millimeters in size to the ragged granite cliffs of a great mountain. This angular form is, however, only characteristic of the original building process. Rocks can be found that are as smooth and rounded as potatoes. But these rounded shapes result from wear and weathering, the changing and removing of material from the mineral form. The potato rocks can be broken to reveal their angular structure within.

As surface tension helps produce the form of the organic cell and so influences plant and animal shapes, in a similar fashion crystallization influences mineral formations.

If a sprinkling of salt is put under low magnification, the individual grains of salt appear. Each is a crystal: translucent, roughly cubic, and varying in size and regularity. They are slightly battered from being shaken about and bear white opaque scratches on their edges and corners. They look somewhat like miniature ice cubes. If a spot of water is dropped on them they immediately become clear as irregularities melt away, leaving a smooth surface, just as ice cubes become clear when immersed. The hard edges and corners disappear next as the salt goes back into solution. The geometric cube quite rapidly becomes a rounded cube, then an amorphous form. As it continues to decrease in size the crystal becomes more and more spherical. The final remnant of the salt crystal is a disappearing speck almost perfectly round.

The little watery solution of salt under the heat of the microscope light soon starts warming and evaporating. The salt cannot evaporate with the water, so as the water becomes scarcer, it becomes supersaturated; the salt must again come out of solution, and the crystals start to rebuild. From minute impurities the crystals grow out in four directions to form four-sided pyramids, built layer by layer on their bases, each layer a perfect square and just slightly smaller than the one preceding it. The new crystals are absolutely square on their corners and flat on their sides, for they only express the mineral formation; they have not yet been exposed to the softening of form in wear. (4)

Granite rock is formed of individual crystals, like salt crystals, bound together. Iron, when cooling and turning from a liquid state into a solid state, forms into crystals, but the crystals are interlocked into a pattern called a lattice. Little space exists between crystals, for like a honeycomb the sides of one nestle tightly into the sides of the other. Granite crystals, though very strong within themselves, are independent in their formation process and so fit together with gaps and holes, a poorer packing job. The form and fit of the constituent parts of a material help determine the characteristics of the material: those with a relatively tight fit are found in the stronger substances, those with loose packing are weaker. When fracture does occur in any crystalline substance the splitting line tends to follow an angular path between the crystals. In either case the cleavage will follow the course of least resistance, the course that is the readiest to separate. The resulting form is flat and angular.

After the organic and mineral forms have been established the decline must begin, with death and dehydration, rot and leaching by the sun and wind. We see the transformation of something in the stages of bud and expansion, growth and gathering to stasis

1-7 A and B Fresh kernels of corn exemplify the tight skin expansion of growing organic form, pushing out on their exterior coverings as growth and liquids accumulate inside. At maturity the growth stops and the forms soon begin to slacken as the liquids of life recede, dehydrate, leach out through the skin and stem. The solid material is left and the remaining liquids are in thick syrup. The once tight covering membrane wrinkles and shrivels to display the characteristic forms of organic aging, typical in the dried apricots and prunes.

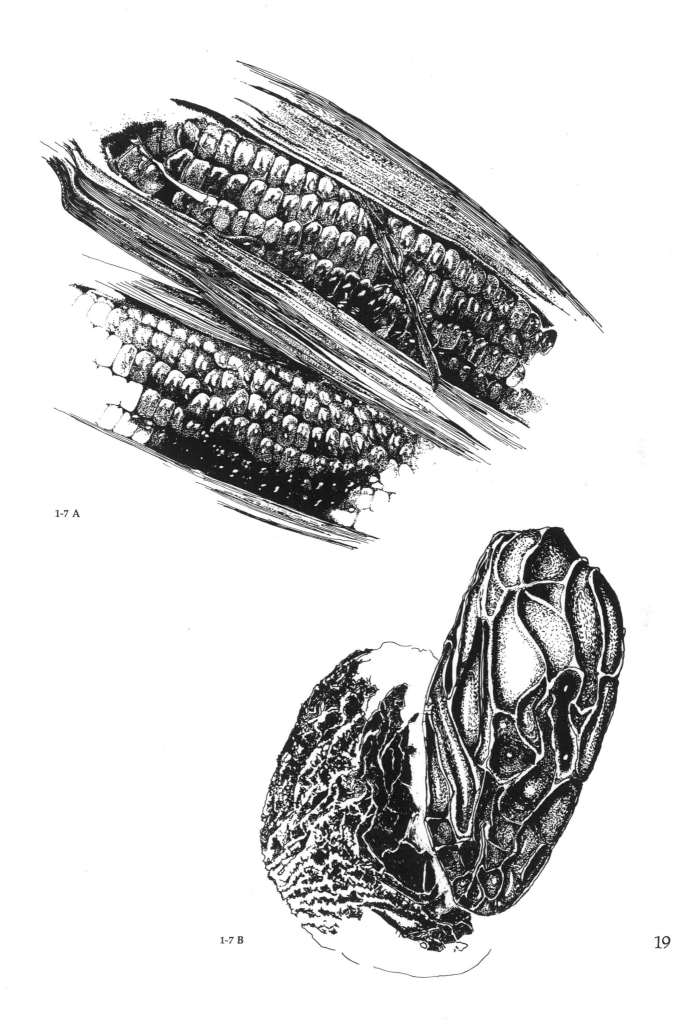

1-7 A

1-7 B

19

and finally the giving up of the material won and developed. These forces of decline exert as much influence on form as do the forces of growth. From the moment the growth process begins and before it ends, the deterioration starts, for there is some aging and decline even in youth. The battering winds lift grains of sand, remove particles of rock, etch wood and dry out resins and oils to leave the organic surface parched and cracked, the inorganic pocked and rounded. With a soft insistent rush oceans and rivers coax away the granite and rust the iron. The rains dissolve and cut into mountainsides and elm leaves with equal efficiency. The sun, insects, animals, fire, rot and ice all work to make less that which chemistry, heat, pressure, time and life have worked to put together. The fragile things must be maintained or left to lead their short lives, the massive things last longer but reveal surfaces and forms that tell of their slow demise, and these forms of diminution can be categorized as distinctly as the forms of growth.

The dehydration of an organic form throughout its mass results in many well-known patterns. The skin is tightly stretched about new growing things as they fill their containers to maximum, but the smooth convex organic surface demands the impossibility of continued expansion to maintain its simple form. The hunger for growth wanes and like a balloon with a slow leak the skin goes slack when the stem no longer pumps in more growth. Dried peas and flesh develop the complex texture of something that pushed its boundaries to the limits but now contracts from within to leave its stretched surface in wrinkles. The surface expands with growth but contracts in folds rather than a lessening of area as the interior grows smaller. The surface becomes loose, no longer associated with the mass it encloses. The thin delicate skin of a new plum has a high gloss to its stretched membrane covering when it is fresh. With dehydration the skin develops fine wrinkles and begins to float on the plum's exterior. As drying continues the skin is slackened more and pushed back upon itself, until finally it becomes the thick, tough, and complex forms of the prune. This process is similar in all dried fruits and vegetables and also animal aging and death, and even with the gathering of film on the surface of a shrinking pond. This is the process of dehydration only from within; the moisture passes from the mass inside through the skin to the outside.

If the organic form grows from the inside, pushing out its skin before it, and retreats from the inside, inorganic is in complete contrast, for it builds from the outside and is diminished from without. The resulting forms are very different. Most of the agents of erosion (wind, water, snow and ice) are usually less hard than the substances upon which they work, the stone and steel and earth.

Removal is often effective only with a lot at a time, for these agents are capable of subtracting just the smallest of particles. At the Vatican in Rome stands a bronze statue of St. Peter. Worshippers have kissed the figure of St. Peter for seven centuries. The statue's right foot has been worn into a smooth deep hollow from only the brush of lips and hands. Each individual in the long procesion of believers has walked away from the statue with a few particles of metal clinging to reverent mouths and fingers. And so it is when the winds and water play about the hard rock cliffs, begging away only particles small enough to manage.

This minute removal process results in a very smooth surface when the material exposed to wear is homogeneous throughout, like the smoothing of salt crystals in water as cited earlier. This same process holds true on a larger scale: sleek boulders worn from the waves' surge, and the molding of very old rotund hills by wind and water. A uniform sand shoreline facing squarely the prevailing wind will give up its banks to erosion in a straight line. A melting sheet of ice across a pond will release its water with an undisturbed smooth surface.

If the surface of the material in erosion is inconsistent, the resulting form is uneven. A gradually eroding coastline of granite set in soft clay produces a complex of shores and bays, peninsulas and islands. The peninsulas and islands are the bolder materials; the bays and inlets are bounded by the easily surrendered substances. A bank of rubble stone eroding to the rain is an etched surface of ridges and spires and deep troughs. Some conglomerate rocks become filled with curved pits and knobs as the hard and soft give way at different rates. Coarse crystalline granite boulders become very rough in wind erosion as the binding material between the crystals gives up early, leaving ragged projections of crystals. After death the more enduring organic materials are often taken with the same erosion process; wood and bone left to the weather for many years reveal their hard and soft grain in ripples and swirls.

Wear is caused by the friction of one substance against another. Each substance in contact and

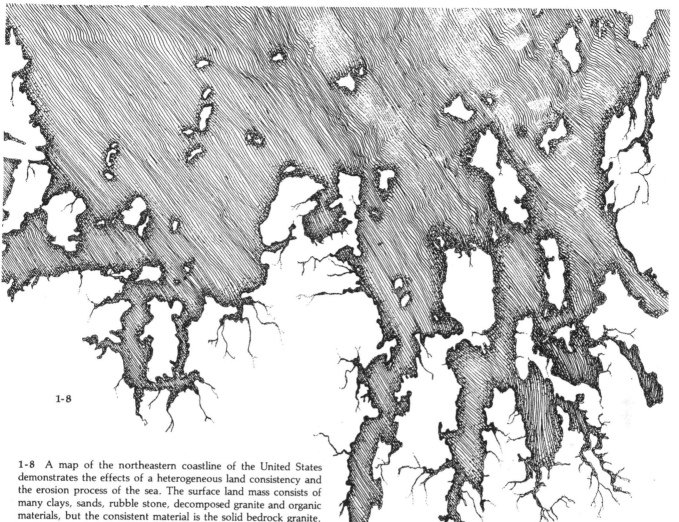

1-8 A map of the northeastern coastline of the United States demonstrates the effects of a heterogeneous land consistency and the erosion process of the sea. The surface land mass consists of many clays, sands, rubble stone, decomposed granite and organic materials, but the consistent material is the solid bedrock granite. In this particular area the prevailing storm force is from a fairly constant southeast direction. The back bays are almost entirely bounded by soft materials, lack granite and are in a moderately rapid state of erosion. The headlands and out-board islands are solid granite monoliths covered only with a sprinkling of soil clinging to the top sides. The overall configuration of the coast is typical of an erosion of heterogeneous material with a constant force regardless of size and scope. A heterogeneous alloy of metal corroding or rusting will display a similar type of surface under magnification.

movement relinquishes a certain quantity of its volume to the tearing action of the other. If wind moves against rock the wind is halted at a point of contact a layer of air of the exact configuration of that of the rock is torn free from the rest of the wind. But in stopping the wind's movement, the minute particles that form the rock's surface, with which the air collides, are themselves broken free.

In this sense all wear is a compromise; both substances compromise at the point of interface. The variables that control the rapidity of erosion or wear are the proportionate quantitites of material passing one another, their speeds, pressures, and hardness.

Gentle breezes can reduce masses of crystalline rock only through vast amounts of time and quantities of air. Water requires less time to wear down rock and the grinding of one rock against another through the earth's shifts rapidly removes material from each.

The direction of the contact movement is another important factor in the determination of these forms of wear. A wiping action, one in which the two substances pass one another in a course parallel to their surfaces, tends to smooth the surface. Hands sliding over a wooden bannister rail, skis moving over new snow, an anchor rope passing around the cleat on a boat — all these actions shear microscopic amounts of material off the high points and deposit them in the ravines, or wear all the material away, and so make the entire surface of one level. The final result is polishing.

When a wearing action takes place in man-made things it is usually the friction occuring between materials that are sliding together; a sock wearing out at the heel between foot and shoe, the soles of the shoe

21

on the ground, the bearings containing rotating parts in machinery, the surface of a well-scrubbed table. (5)

With movement between touching surfaces wearing is unavoidable. The choice is which surface should relinquish its material to a greater degree. A consideration of the compatibility between two dissimilar materials in contact is essential. Machine bearings are deliberately made of soft lead or bronze alloy to aid lubrication and to be worn away, for the bearing is far easier to replace than the shaft rotating inside it. The ideal machine would be frictionless and so without any wear at all. The goal is to contain the moving part so that its travel is uniform but to prevent it from touching any other surface. (6)

A sheet of glass to our fingers feels very even and slick, but smoothness is relative. A fly can walk up a window pane with ample footholds in the glass' minutely coarse surface. Any material pursued far enough into the microscopic recesses of its surface is revealed as craggy and rough. It is this roughness that speeds wear.

When two surfaces are in contact, the burr of one surface interlocks with the other, as fingers clasped together; the greater the pressure pushing the surfaces together the greater the areas of contact as the "outs" of one surface press further into the "ins" of the other. For this reason pressure is an extremely important factor in wear. When two surfaces that are held firmly together are moved in opposition to each other, or rubbed together, the meshed surface burr of each surface is sheared off and a new surface burr is exposed, and the process repeats. The smoother surfaces intrude on each other less. In theory two infinitely smooth surfaces in contact would have no wear at all, for the two surfaces would not penetrate one another, but would remain separated, parallel and frictionless. (7)

In practice, a very rough surface will wear faster than one that has been smoothed. A tire squealing to a stop will achieve it faster on a rough macadam road

1-9   A greatly enlarged sectional view taken of the intersection of two steel parts held firmly together without any lubrication between. The irregular blocks are molecules. Steel is a highly heterogeneous substance consisting of hard and soft areas, granules, impurities, a matrix of graphite, ferrite, carbon, and other elementary particles depending upon the blend and purity. This mixed composition results in the vast range of properties of iron and steel. The surface of these contacting parts in the drawing is considered to be polished for normal machine use. The actual area of contact between the two pieces is very small, so consequently each protuberance supports an enormous force even in a moderate loading. Often these small contact points will "weld" together from the pressure and heat caused by friction. If these two surfaces were to travel in different directions, an enormous tearing action would result, rending molecules and granules out of place, rolling them between the moving surfaces and tearing more loose. The friction builds temperature, which adds to surface deterioration. These are the conditions of surface-to-surface wear without lubrication.

1-9

than a smooth concrete one because of greater friction, but will wear much faster as the ruffled road surface tears more rubber away from the tire. Rain on an even concrete roadway fills the depressions and glazes the surface; the water in effect turns the road's rough surface into a fine textured one. A tire traveling rapidly over the wet pavement lifts off the concrete and makes contact only with the water and high points of the roadway. The interlocking of rubber and water has little friction, for it can be easily sheared, a very undesirable condition for the safety of the driver. However, if the only concern were the wear on the tire, the water would be beneficial, for with the addition of this third substance between the tire and road, the advantages of lubrication—the major inhibitor of friction and wear—have been achieved.

Lubricants penetrate these minutely rough surfaces and build a cushion between the two materials in contact. This cushion not only makes the surface in contact very smooth by leveling the ins and outs, but also compromises the movement from both sides. (8)

Most wear associated with man's actions and his devices comes about from this parallel surface movement. But there are two other less common types of wearing and erosion found in a natural and manmade state. The first of these is one that is primarily in a direction perpendicular to the surface. The second is one that is multidirectional. A hammer pounding on a steel anvil, rain falling straight down on rock in the absence of wind, a wind storm flinging grains of sand into the windshield of a a car: these are examples of a situation of perpendicular wear. Unlike the parallel movement, this kind of action etches and roughens the surface. Metal separates in flakes when pounded; rain can scar rock over a long period of time with tiny pockmarks; and a blast of sand can score and etch almost any hard surface very rapidly. Much the same result can be achieved by water and chemicals dissolving perpendicularly into mineral surfaces, and so etching a roughness into them; but insects and fire also effect the same result as they remove material unevenly by entering directly into the substance. Perpendicular wear can be found in some large scale examples as well.

The agents of erosion are not always uniform in the direction of their movement upon the materials. They often can come about from any direction, as in multi-directional wear. A granite outcropping facing the surge of an exposed coastline will compromise its

1-10 A

1-10 A and B If it were possible to have a close look at the contact point between a tire surface and a smooth dry cement roadway, it might look something like the first drawing, a situation of fairly good contact between the high points of the road surface and the tire. In a dry state the tread allows the tire surface to deform to better match the road surface configuration. The second drawing depicts a wet condition at a high speed of tire travel. The surface of the tire actually rides up on the water, only making contact with the high points of the roadway. This action is called hydroplaning. In this situation the treads act as a water escape, helping to drain off the surface water. The water has the same action as a lubricant.

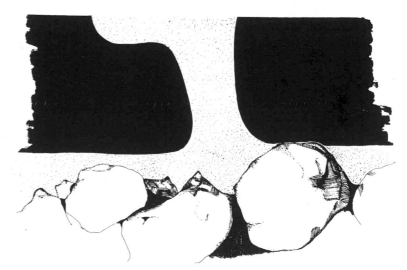

1-10 B

mineral form with that of the wave action and so display smooth sculptural concave and convex shapes that result from the multidirectional lashing of the waves. Feet scurrying this way and that, sliding, scuffling, pounding over a busy curbstone; and hands working over the turnstiles, knewelposts, straps, and handles of public places express the random action of multidirectional wearing. Machines

23

1-11 A

1-11 A and B The purpose of lubrication is to reduce the surface to surface contact of moving parts by interposing a layer that is not easily penetrated and has a low shear strength, or is, to varying degrees, viscous. The phrase "reduce contact" is used because no common lubricants are truly successful; there are always irregularities that penetrate the lubricant and make contact with the opposing surface and instantaneously "weld" together. Lubricant failure is caused by the force of the two surfaces coming together. This force varies from point to point. Local high temperature and sliding velocities also cause film breakdown.

There are three common types of lubrication: boundary, thin film, and hydrodynamic. This illustration shows two: "A" is Boundary, and "B" is Hydrodynamic. The third type, thin film, is a combination of boundary and hydrodynamic. Boundary (A) depends on minute quantities of lubricant coating the moving parts. It is used with most fast moving machinery such as car engines. Boundary lubrication is usually a thin oil. Hydrodynamic lubrication (B) builds up a volume of fluid that physically separates the moving parts under pressure. Hydrodynamic lubrication is used in slower moving parts such as the steering and suspension of a car and farm machinery. The lubricant used is a thick grease which will remain in place.

Both of these lubricants make movement easier by leveling off the imperfections, which effects a smoother surface. If two microscopically perfect surfaces (a practical impossibility) came in contact, no lubrication would be necessary for they would slide friction-free on their smooth surfaces.

Dry lubricants such as graphite and talc are essentially the same as boundary. The molecules of these lubricants are of very fine grain. They smear between the two moving parts and help to prevent microwelds by coating the parts. Some types of metal, such as grey iron, contain enough graphite to give the metal an inherent wear resistance.

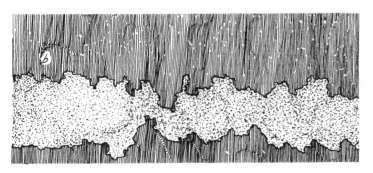

1-11 B

rarely show this wear, for little is random in mechanical movement.

All materials have their own idiomatic characteristics. The idiom of the material is a request to the user of that material to understand its personal identity and meaning, its strengths and weaknesses, its structure, its comfortable forms and its best use.

A worker with a long intimate association with a material can often comprehend the idiom of that material more completely than the physicist, chemist, or materials engineer. The trained specialists may be versed in properties and composition but not be able to feel by hand the exact amount of torque to put on a quarter inch steel bolt to hold it very tight but just short of shearing. A material can be catalogued and defined, its properties analyzed and its structure recognized, but this kind of determination cannot replace the empirical knowledge that is developed by the experienced hand working through years of direct friendship with the material. The mind and the hand know just when and how to best use a section of wood or a piece of iron. Strength, weight, and structure are determined with empirical accuracy, though the builder may not be able to verbalize in technical terms an approximation of what has been built.

One hundred and fifty years ago, wood and forged iron set the foundations for the industrialized era to follow. They were king and queen then with a rather homey quality, for they ruled the domain of the local blacksmith, wagonwright, cooper, ship's chandler, farmer and many others who built and repaired implements of these materials; many came to know them well. On countless workbenches in farmers' lean-to sheds pitched behind the barn could be found tools of forged iron and wood for repair and construction: a newly forged chain hook, a wooden shovel handle broken at the knot, a kitchen chair with hickory legs and a seat of elm set on the bench for tightening and re-wedging after several dry seasons. A wooden moldboard plow on the bench for construction — the curving draft beam was cut from a long bent oak limb with a forked branch cut intact to serve as a very strong "Y" connection between two structural parts on the plow. These forms responded to the most critical needs and advantages of the materials. The two materials, iron and wood, are associated in many ways.

The most significant similarity is that both have a grain that comes about through their development and gives them toughness in their uses by man. The

1-12

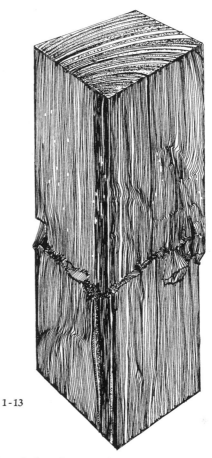

1-13

1-12 Wrought iron and cut timber were the basic materials of early industrial production. They were strong, durable, available and easily worked. Most rural communities developed their own products by themselves from these materials. Some rural artisans developed to a high degree the craft of working wood and iron. Many such craftsmen could be found in the Shaker communities.

This latch is a simple but elegant statement of wrought iron artisanship. The Shaker ironsmith who made it not only understood the need of its function as a product, but the qualities of the way the iron works, its strengths and its best forms.

1-13 Grain is the secret of strength in many things. Pictured is a 4″ x 4″ section of spruce wood 10″ long that was put under a compressive force of eighty thousand pounds. Each column of vertical grain acted as a small pillar, and each reinforced the other laterally. When failure came it started at a weak point and rapidly spread horizontally, each column of grain bending and breaking at three points to result in a pleated effect that reduced the total length of the wood three-sixteenths of an inch. In any situation where the parts that come together have a fibrous structure, or a "grain," the intersection is increased in strength when the fibers align to the linear direction of the form, or the fibers reflect the shape of the form.

grain of forged iron corresponds to that particular forged shape and the grain of wood corresponds in its growth to the tree's dendritic pattern.

Understanding a material's grain structure is essential to understanding the material. As the substances of earth flow from one form into another, they leave paths within their structure that reveal the course of

their travel and the change of their shape. A glacier or a landslide can be seen from above with lines of movement running parallel to the direction of their flow. These lines are caused by various foreign substances and irregularities picked up en route; their effect is stretched over the length of the substance in movement. The grain of wood and forged iron flows into their forms in a similar fashion. Were a large fully matured tree to be sliced in half parallel to its length from the tips of its branches through its trunk and into its roots, the flow of its grain would be seen to follow its silhouette. This cross-section exposes the grain in its paralleled movement from the roots up through the bole and major branches into the twigs. It is this grain that gives the tree, and the wooden products made from the tree, their strength.

The artisans and craftsmen of years past who worked with wood recognized this structural quality and used it to their advantage to a greater degree than woodworkers today. Not only did they know how to place the grain in flat sections, but they used the natural curves of the tree to form the curves in their products. When intersections were needed, they often and whenever possible formed them from the intersections of branches. The result of this kind of

25

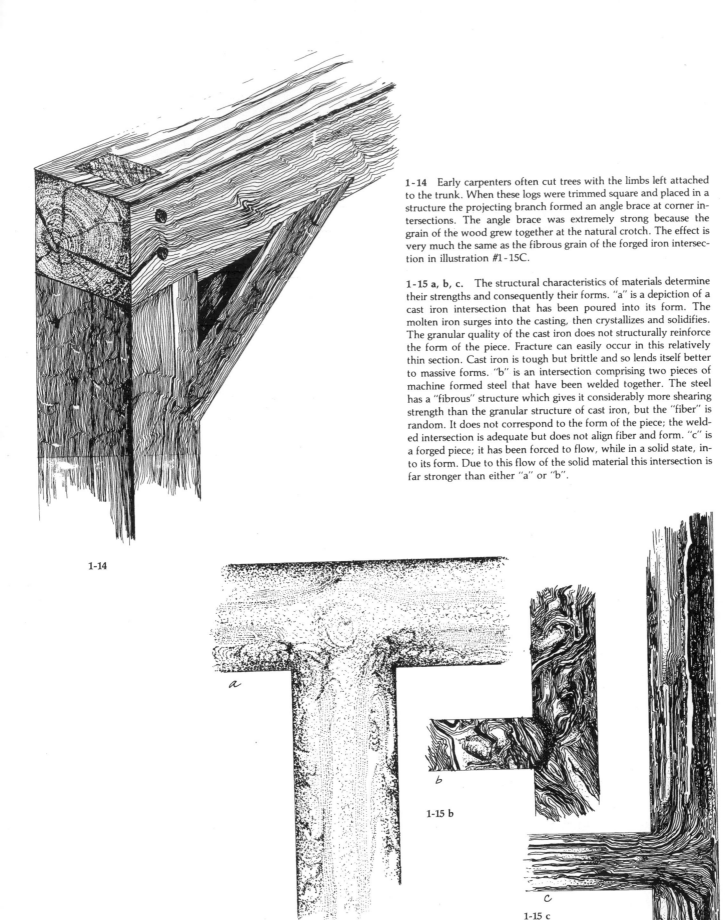

1-14 Early carpenters often cut trees with the limbs left attached to the trunk. When these logs were trimmed square and placed in a structure the projecting branch formed an angle brace at corner intersections. The angle brace was extremely strong because the grain of the wood grew together at the natural crotch. The effect is very much the same as the fibrous grain of the forged iron intersection in illustration #1-15C.

1-15 a, b, c. The structural characteristics of materials determine their strengths and consequently their forms. "a" is a depiction of a cast iron intersection that has been poured into its form. The molten iron surges into the casting, then crystallizes and solidifies. The granular quality of the cast iron does not structurally reinforce the form of the piece. Fracture can easily occur in this relatively thin section. Cast iron is tough but brittle and so lends itself better to massive forms. "b" is an intersection comprising two pieces of machine formed steel that have been welded together. The steel has a "fibrous" structure which gives it considerably more shearing strength than the granular structure of cast iron, but the "fiber" is random. It does not correspond to the form of the piece; the welded intersection is adequate but does not align fiber and form. "c" is a forged piece; it has been forced to flow, while in a solid state, into its form. Due to this flow of the solid material this intersection is far stronger than either "a" or "b".

1-14

1-15 b

1-15 c

1-15 a

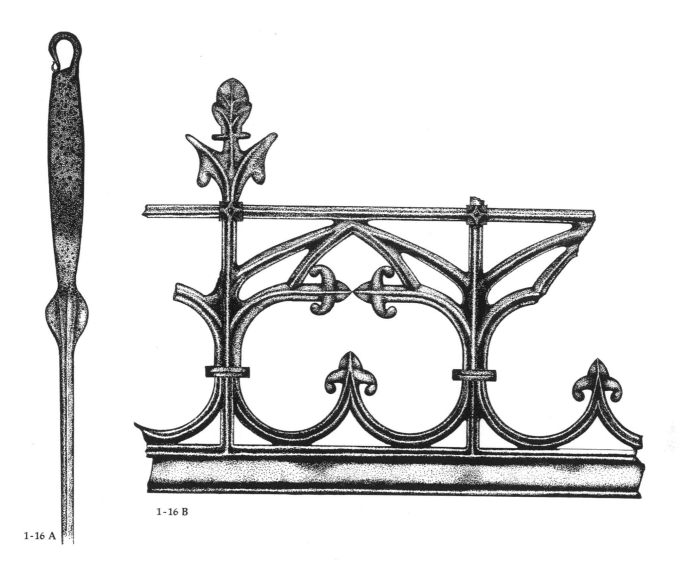

1-16 A

1-16 B

1-16 A and B A blacksmith pounded this poker handle from a solid iron bar into this pleasant curving form in a good example of the workability of wrought iron. Contrast this form with the form of the cast iron fence in Illustration #1-16B. Both express the idiom of the material from which they are made. The wrought iron poker is a good form for the material; the cast iron fence is not as appropriate.

Depicted is a section of an old cast iron cemetery fence. These fences were originally copies of Spanish and Moroccan wrought iron work. Though the wrought iron was tougher and more resistant to breakage, it rusted rapidly in the damp northern countries. The cast iron fence was resistant to rust, but was very brittle in these thin sections, and so not rust but breakage ended the fence's life.

building let the paths of grain flow into each other where the parts joined like the intersecting stream of two rivers. Iron that is formed by the pounding of the blacksmith's hammer also flows into its shape and so will have a grain that echoes its exterior form like the layers on an onion.

Modern materials have even more need to be understood, for the mistakes no longer are limited to a single item but are multiplied by mass production.

The materials are often more complex and the methods of working them are massive and sophisticated. Forged iron is seldom used now, but the backsmith's trade has endured through translation. The iron has become steel, the products are automobile bodies rather than sleigh runners, and the hammer blows come from a stamping press, but the metal still flows; this ability of steel to flow has made the Iron Age possible.

A twenty-thousand-ton stamping press reaches eighty-five miles an hour in descent to bring two matching dies together with a flat sheet of steel between. During that split second descent, the leading curve of the male die strikes the material being formed and the steel sheet wrinkles, deforming into a pocket, the wrinkles compound and eddy across the surface. The waves grow smaller and multiply again in number. The two dies then touch the upper and lower crests of the waves, flatten them out, push them in and throw the surging tide of metal back into itself to flow molecularly and redistribute its volume within the stretched smooth, contoured thickness; the cold metal flows. The dies separate and a new car hood is ready for paint. An ingot of red hot steel 4 feet thick and 8 feet long is run back and forth under the rollers of a forming press until it flows into a sheet one-sixteenth of an inch thick and hundreds of feet long.

Of all the modern materials, plastics remain the enigma. Unfortunately the most prevalent quality that designers and manufacturers have settled upon and so used most is the ability of plastics to copy traditional and more expensive materials.

The following two paragraphs relate identical situations. The first is the intended conception; the second is the reality:

The customer sits at his luncheon bar. His seat is a deep black leather bar stool. Elbows rest on a highly polished cherrywood bar counter. Fingers reach for peanuts in a small oaken bucket banded with brass straps and raise for a sip a chipped crystal glass. Beneath him the intricate hardwood parquet spans the floor to the stained glass windows, and above, hand-hewn oak beams cross the whitewashed ceilings. A black plastic telephone nestles behind the bar.

The customer sits at his luncheon bar. His seat is a styrofoam and vinyl leather-grained bar stool. Elbows rest on a luster finish cherry-grained masonite bar counter. Fingers reach for peanuts in a high density crinkle-finished polypropylene bucket decaled with vacuum-metalized polyurethane straps, and raise for a sip an injection-molded clear styrene glass. Beneath him the wood-grained vinyl flooring reaches the amber acrylic panels; above, pressure-formed textured-surface urethane beams span the textured sheet rock ceiling. A black plastic telephone nestles behind the bar.

Only the telephone in these impressions is true to its material, for it has no tradition leading to its contemporary form that it must copy. In this setting of imitation and dishonesty, finishes have been copied and forms have been executed with dazzling fidelity. One must often reach out and touch the material to be assured of suspicions. The glue-on urethane beams that lace the ceiling certainly do appear to be the real thing. And so we are faced with the question: does it really matter whether the beams are real or not if the wanted effect is achieved? Part of the answer lies with the disdain that is expressed for the honest association built by the craftsmen working with their

materials, and part lies with the potential not realized, the idiom not explored.

Plastics have become the great imitators, for they can appear as wood or steel, brass or leather. Often plastic is more successful than that which it is imitating. But the greatest crime in the dishonest use of plastic lies not as much in the attempts to make it become another material but in the disregard for its own complex idiom. Like the natural materials, plastic has its own set of rules, its formulae of manufacture that regulate its qualities.

One-fifth of the world's population walks in plastic shoes. Throughout dozens of countries the poor can buy white polypropylene sandals for a few pennies. In one manufacturing process, one injection-molding shot, the soles, straps and fasteners are formed. They last longer than leather in all kinds of conditions and can be duplicated by no other material as simply. Plastic can copy other materials, but no other material can do all that plastic can. If the roles were reversed and plastic were taken to be a natural material, perhaps mined by the ancients but coming into scarcity now, and bronze were a newly developed material and in lavish quantity, the manufacturers would very probably be attempting, with considerable difficulty, to make bronze appear plastic-like.

Paper, glass, sand, smoke, and all other materials whether used by man or not have a particular grouping of characteristics that make them individual. Natural materials vary not only from type to type, wood to stone, but also change character from each individual section to section. Each tree is different from all the rest, and within the trunk and limbs the variety is continued. The roots are sinuous, the outside of the trunk is soft pliable wood; the heart wood is stronger; the crotch wood is very tough where the tree has built up strength to hold a long limb in a horizontal position.

The forces on any structure, especially a moving one, vary considerably from point to point. Some parts require flexibility; others require rigidity. An aluminum beam in the wing of an airplane is uniform in composition throughout its length though it is subject to very different requirements of load from the ends to the middle. Aeronautical engineers have not solved this problem of structure to load as well as nature has in various animal long bones. Most animal leg bones require a flexibility at the two ends and comparative rigidity in the center of the shaft. A rapid glance at the bones' structure reveals a marvelous combination of flexibility moving into rigidity. The theory behind this has an inorganic analogy. A solid glass rod is quite rigid, and will break easily if bent, but the same amount of glass in the form of fine threads will make a rope which has the tensional strength of the original rod plus flexibility and can be tied into a knot without breaking. Just so the system of the bony trabeculae near the ends of the bone provides mechanical support combined with flexibility; toward the center of the long bone the flexibility gradually gives way to rigidity.

The way in which the materials of earth come together to best resist the forces of their environment is what determines structure. And in turn, structure is the most immediate determinant of form.

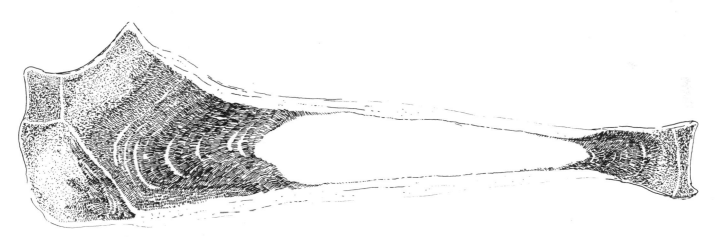

1-17

1-17 Animal structure and material is often of more sophisticated compostion than its manmade counterpart. The structure of bone is a harmony of force absorption. The fibers (trabeculae) that constitute the hard sections of bone align themselves to the stress. The shape of long bones is tubular, a form which offers a high strength/weight ratio. Inside the hard bony shell the substance moves from quite hard and rigid near the central shaft (diaphysis) to very soft at the extreme ends, providing the necessary rigidity at the central shaft and the necessary absorption of shock and stress at the ends. This graduation is shown in the drawing above of a human ulna, which is typical of vertebrate skeleton long bones. The graduation from soft to hard is expressed in the following materials: at the socket joint the movement is lubricated with synovial fluid, a viscous medium that lubricates and absorbs shock. The socket is lined with hyaline cartilage, a soft spongy babbitting, saturated with synovial fluid. Calcified cartilage backs up the hyaline cartilage. It is a tougher material, stiffened with mineral salts. Subchondral bone then moves into the shaft. The subchondral bone is yielding and spongy, but harder than the cartilage.

2 STRUTS AND TIES
The Elements of Structure

In the forest the trees grow tall, thin and straight in their competitive attempt to reach the sunlight; on the open field the tree's form is short and rounded by the full swing of the sun. The tree's circumstances help control its form but it is the tree's material and structure that must hold its form intact against the force of the elements, the wind, rain, snow and gravity.

In the long limbs the fibers of wood on the upper surface are in tension as gravity pulls the limb downward, and the fibers on the bottom side of the limb are compressed together. Torsion occurs inside the wood as gravity pulls curving limbs; shear is found in the movement between the fibers of wood as the wind sways the branches and trunks about, bending them this way and that.

With these five forces: tension, compression, torsion, shear, and bending, the tree is re-enacting an old theme, one that runs through every form that must contend with a force anywhere on earth. The theme is called structure and it can be defined in the following way. Structure is the way to achieve the most strength from the least material, through the most appropriate arrangement of elements within the best form for the intended use, and constructed from the material most suited to the kind of stress placed upon it.

Structure is focused in one direction: getting the very most from the very least. Structure is not making something strong by building mass and volume, but rather, using less material in the most appropriate way, thereby achieving strength, only adding more material when the existing elements have been used to their fullest extent. Structure is economy. But economy in this sense is not just frugality. Without the economy of structure the bird could not fly, nor the airplane, for they would fall to earth from their own weakness or great weight. Without economy of materials the bridge could not hold its own weight, nor could the tree. The very large and light, the very

2-1 This tree was broken by the pressure of the wind, and in so doing revealed three major forces of stress. The lower section and roots of the tree resisted the pressure of the wind in the upper branches. When failure occurred, it came in the middle of the trunk. A large break was torn open on the windward side; the fibers of wood were actually pulled apart in *tension* as the break opened up. The other side acted as a hinge; there the wood was *compressed*. The pulling on one side resulted in pushing on the other side. Between the two was a neutral zone, neither in compression nor tension. This is the area where *shear* and bending takes place, a sliding action is present, one force sliding past the other.

2-2 Because of exaggerated forces in large objects, complex structures like bridges must be extremely carefully considered for the utmost economy of form. Only the material that is "working" to maximum should be there, and certainly no superfluous material. The builders of the Firth of Forth Railway Bridge over the Tay River made these kinds of decisions. Each member and its placement had to be considered for economy, for adding weight necessitated more structure. All the compression members are tubular and all the tension members are open lattice girders. As with all structures of economy, the members are specialized to their tasks.

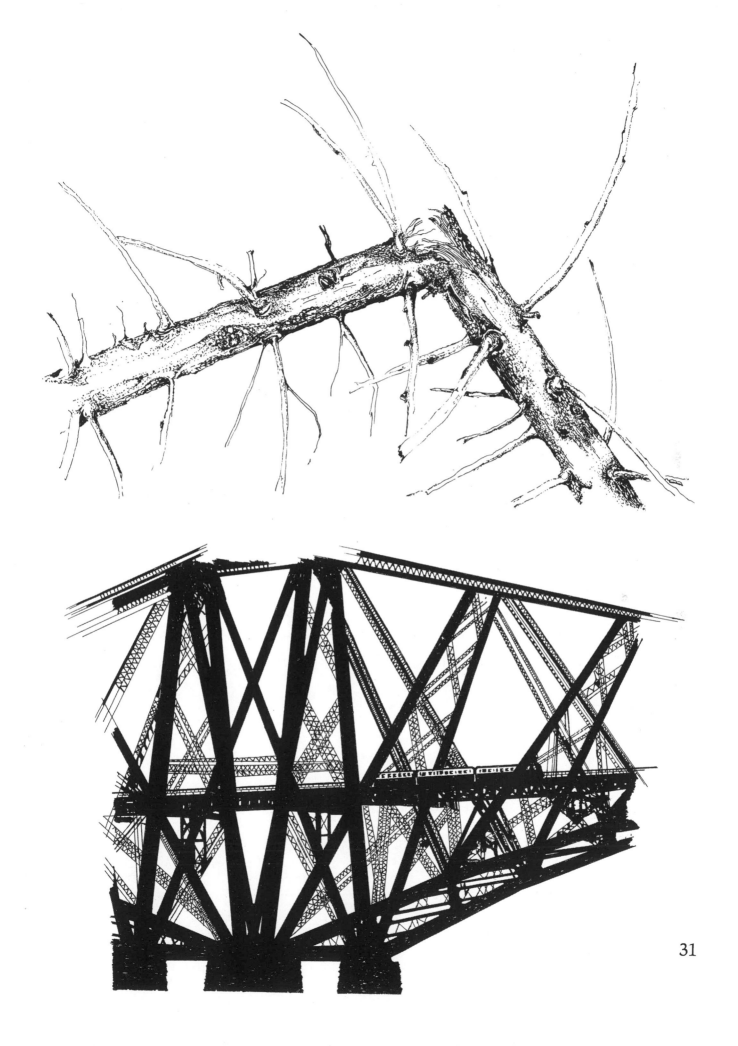

31

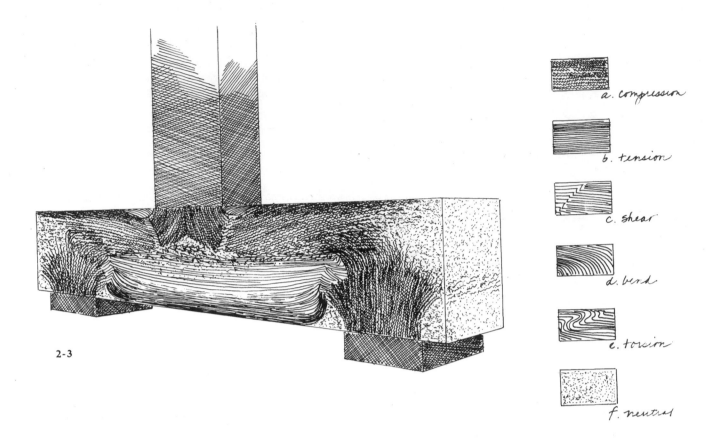

2-3

a. *compression*

b. *tension*

c. *shear*

d. *bend*

e. *torsion*

f. *neutral*

strong and fast demand the most from structure. Economy begins to take on an entirely different meaning when applied to an enormous structure like the multi-million pound Firth of Forth Railroad Bridge in Scotland. The bridge uses 145 acres of steelwork, yet was constructed under stringent demands of economy of materials.

The primary function of a kite, airplane or a bird is to stay aloft, supported only by air. In order to accomplish this with the least effort, the material from which the flying object or organism is constructed must be light yet provide for the strength requirements. It must have strength enough to withstand maximum violent action within bounds, but not more, for over-structuring would mean an additional weight burden of unused material, and thus hamper the function. The strength/weight ratio is not of so much concern in the case of an elephant or an office building, and so they can afford to be over-burdened with heavier but less structurally specialized materials, presenting less of a construction problem.

It can be said that, although never found, there is a perfect structural form for every task. However, because each material and quality of material, kind of load and condition of environment, is different, the perfect structure can only be determined when all the variables are accounted for.

2-3 If it were possible to see the resolution of forces inside a beam that was supported at each end and loaded in the center, the result would appear like this. Compression fans build up inside each point of contact, then radiate in shear which joins a band of tension across the bottom. The compression is most intense just adjacent to the outside forces and along the extreme lower side between the supporting pier. This is where failure would most likely appear. Both tension and compression lose intensity as they move to the center where a band of neutrality interfaces them. The ends of the beam are relatively neutral as are other small pockets between the streams of force. Shear is found where opposing forces meet.

2-4 This illustration was drawn from a polarized photograph showing the intersection of two forms; the vertical column is pushing down upon the horizontal member. The forces are strongest at the corners and diminish in radial rings in the horizontal member. A more complex situation is seen in the vertical member. A compression circle develops in the center just about the point of contact. This holds the majority of pressure to the outside edges. It might be interesting to speculate as to the type of form that would develop if the design were to follow the distribution of force, rather than a generalized form, such as a cylinder or rectangle.

2-5 A similar situation to that in Drawing 2-4, the beam here is held in a cantilevered position, the triangle indicating the point of weight. Tension and compression are not indicated in these drawings; however, they are fairly easy to place. The points of greatest force are the lower outside corner and the upper inside corner. The top of the cantilevered beam is in tension, the bottom in compression. There are also many points of shear and torsional forces as the horizontal beam tries to rotate out of its position.

Within any structural system there is an infinite number of factors which can determine the form with

32

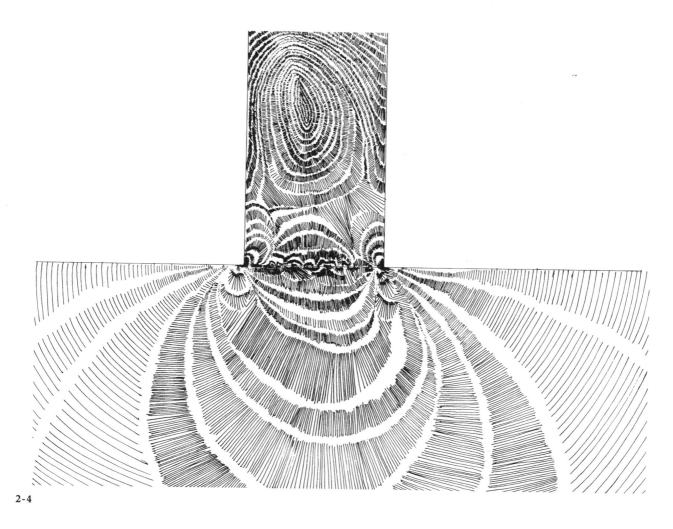

2-4

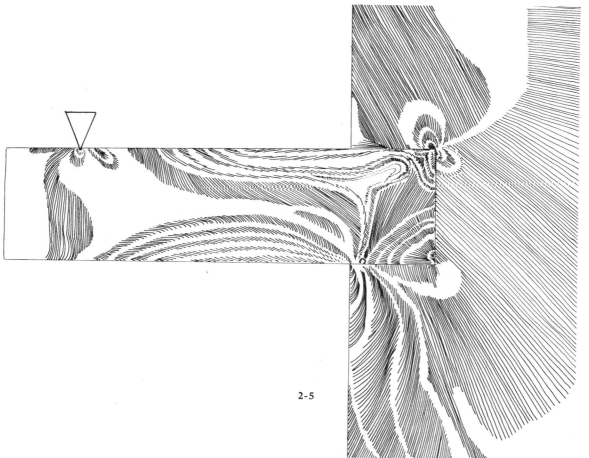

2-5

33

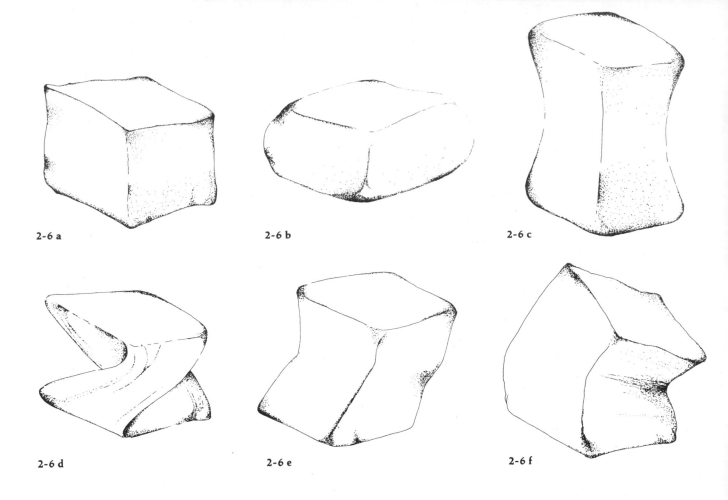

2-6 a   2-6 b   2-6 c

2-6 d   2-6 e   2-6 f

the best potential for precise resolution. If a given weight were to be placed in the center of a solid rectilinear wooden beam which in turn was supported at each end, the beam would carry the load out to its ends, where it would be transferred downward. If it were decided that the beam could be lightened considerably and still support its load, from where would material best be removed? Or to put it another way, what parts of the beam are doing most of the work, and what factors would have to be considered in the removal of material?

If it were possible to determine exactly the right amount of material to be removed to diminish the bulk of the beam to that just capable of holding the dead load and no more, then we would have to consider such factors as all the slight and greater imperfections in the woods, its grain length, direction, and the inner cellular variation, the beam length, depth, and height, the spread of the load, the area of footing on each side, the varying ability of the wood to resist tension, compression and shear in different parts of the beam, and many more classifications of factors. This complexity would be compounded if a live or moveable and varying load had to be considered. It can be seen that the end form resulting from this kind

2-6 a, b, c, d, e, f. Imagine a flexible soft rubber cube to demonstrate the five major stress forces: a) the cube as it is without any stress upon it; b) squashed in compression; c) stretched in tension; d) twisted in torsion; e) bisected by two shearing forces; f) turned by bending forces.

of removal structuring will be very complicated, nonuniform, and in a practical sense, impossible.

The method, however impractical, is still valid. The structure that would evolve responds only to its load and material. It is a three dimensional diagram of weight distribution and transfer, a column of material placed only where it is needed and aligned to the direction of stress, and the material equated to the kind of stress. This is the basis for the perfect structure.

A triangulated trusswork bridge is the result of the same kind of building practice; the calculations, though, are completed on paper before construction. The uniformity of the trusswork bridge makes the structure cruder, for it is generalized for practical

2-7 A and B Unlike the umbrella and the bicycle wheel (which are self-contained tension structures) the spiderweb is a tension structure that is dependent upon its surroundings. The whole of the web is in tension, but it relies on the things about it to hold it that way. The Brooklyn Bridge also is a tension structure that relies upon the land about it to hold it in its position of stretched tension.

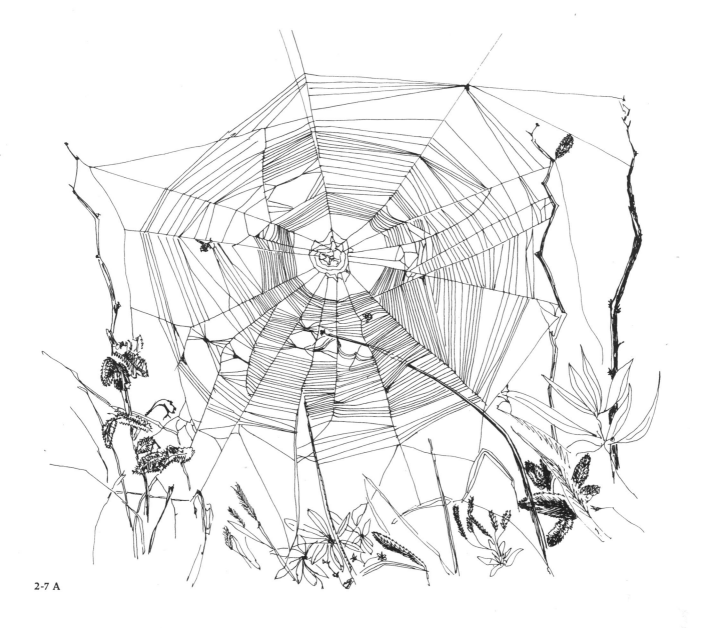

2-7 A

2-7 B

considerations. The structure created from the beam varied tremendously from part to part, each area of the form responded to localized needs. (9)

In all structures the forces of stress are the same: compression, tension, torsion, shear, and bending. Before examining the other aspects of structure it might be well to investigate these five forces to understand how they regulate structure and form so definitively.

Compression is the simplest and most basic of these stresses. Compression is the direct expression of gravity pulling everything to the center of the earth. In compression the waters quickly flow to the earth's low places and the soils hug the earth's crust, always creeping downwards. Gravity holds most of man's structures tightly together in compression. Columns, posts, piers, pylons and walls rise vertically from the ground in compression to hold the horizontal members, the bridges and lintels, the rafters and floors away from the earth. Compression is also produced by the tightening edges of a bolt or clamp or in the squeezing of a peg inside a hole. Of all the forces, compression is the most easily understood. The architectural as well as the natural forms that asssume mostly compressive loads are usually thick and short: the elephant leg and the marble column. The reason for this we will examine soon.

The forms of tension are completely opposite, for tension is in opposition to compression; where there is one there must be the other. The qualities of tension structures are expressed in such forms as spiderwebs, umbrellas, sailboats, suspension bridges, and bicycle wheels. Tension structures are thin, light and often linear in appearance. Many materials, such as wire and fabric, can be used only in tensional loading.

The spokes on a bicycle wheel are in tension pulling the outside rim into the center. The rim is in compression. The bicycle wheel is a self-contained tension/compression structure. A spiderweb is in tension but it is not self-contained for it relies on the outside environment to hold it tight. An umbrella is opposite to a bicycle wheel; the spokes on the umbrella push out in compression and the fabric on the outside holds it tight while it is in tension. The parachute and balloon are tension structures without solid compression members. The air or gas inside the tension membrane acts as the compression element. (10)

Some structures have a majority of their members in tension and others have mostly compression members. Those with a majority of compression members, compression structures, are not as strong pound for pound as tension structures. By way of an explanation, presume that a steel bar 1/2″ in diameter used as a small column 1 foot long is capable of supporting a weight of 1000 pounds in compression before it bends and buckles. A steel bar also of 1/2″ diameter and five times as long has a carrying capacity of only 250 pounds, and a 1/2″ steel bar 100 feet long would be far short of holding its own weight before it buckled. The same bar of steel 1/2″ in diameter used in tension, however, or hanging its load, would be able to hold the 1000 pounds at a length of 2 feet, 4 feet, 10 feet, 100 feet, and would lose no supporting capacity. Tensional strength does not diminish as the length grows greater. Tensional structures such as suspension bridges and hung roofs can attain enormous proportions and still be constructed with slender members. Compression structures must become proportionately heavier in girth as they become bigger. (11)

Tension and compression are the two pure forms of stress and are the basis for the other three: shear, bending, and torsion. Shear is a complex stress—it can result from compression and tension in various combinations. When two forces are thrusting in opposite directions but offset and slide past each other, shear is present. As the earth's continental shelves move about, great shearing forces grind between the earth's crust and the land masses. When earthquakes rumble, subterranean plates shift, tension and compression build and faults snap, relieving the pressure but shearing the land and carrying all above in op-

2-8 One of the important laws of structure is found when dealing with size in relationship to structural bulk. Large compression structures must be much thicker and heavier in proportion to smaller ones. There can be found a practical limit to the size of compression structures, for they get so bulky that they exceed common building practices. Tension structures do not have constraints. It should be noted that by compression structures the reference is to those structures with the large majority (or all) of their members in compression, and tension structures are those with a majority of major elements in tension. The drawing is given to help explain this phenomenon. There are two rows of weights; the bottom row is held up by rods placed on stands; the top row is hung from above. The supporting rods in all cases are the same diameter. It can be seen in the bottom row of weights, held up by compression, that as the rod increases in length the size of the weight must be cut in half to avoid bending and buckling. The stand to the bottom right supports 1,000 lbs. one foot off the ground. A rod three times that long can only support 500 lbs. and so on until the rod cannot even support its own weight without bending to the ground. In the top row, however, the weights are hung by rods, and the length of rod and size of weight can double many times over without any buckling, for it cannot occur in a tensional force. Hence tension bridges are the longest structures built.

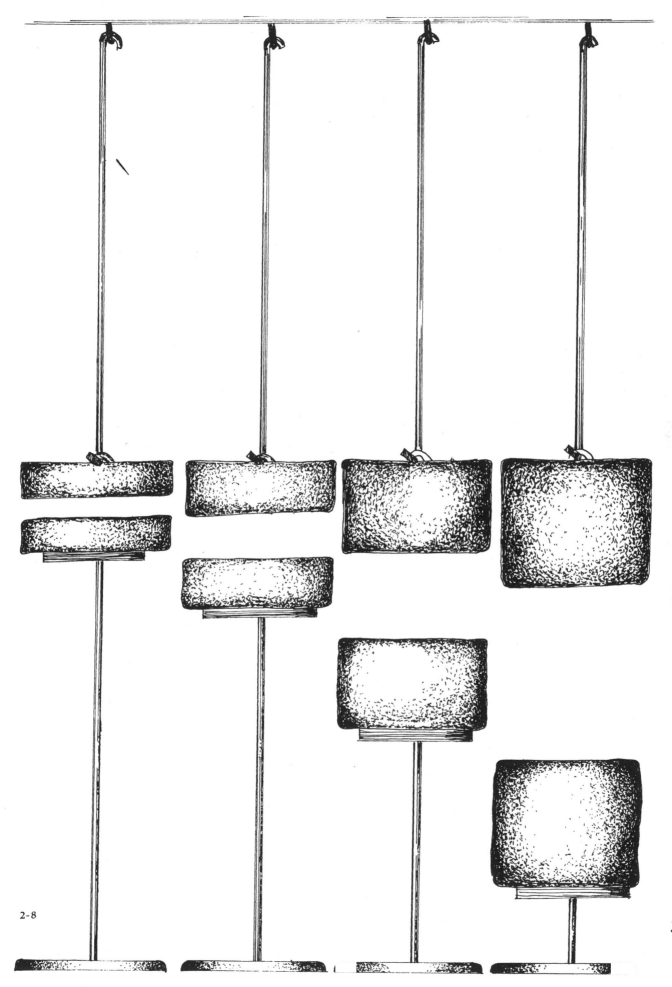

2-9

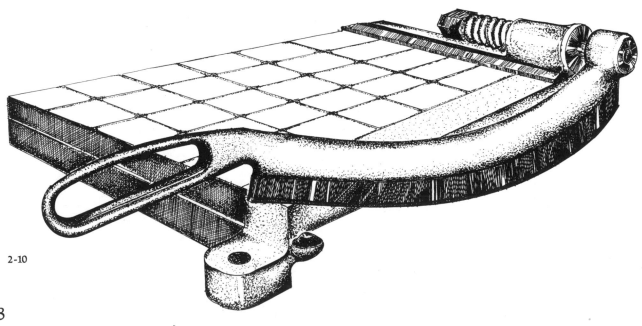

2-10

38

posite directions. Shearing is an alignment to a force from one direction. Faults and cracks form parallel to the direction of the force that caused them. The wind moving through a grassland, the ocean wave rushing over rockweed, and a comb being run through hair are also expressions of shear, as elements respond to forces of movements lining them up. Shear is also present when one is rubbing hands together and shearing paper with a pair of scissors, or sliding an arm into a coat.

In structural concerns, shear and bending are found between the pulling of tension and the pushing of compression. Imagine a deck of cards held between finger and thumb of one hand. If the hand closes, compressing the deck together, it will bend, and while in a bent position, it will be noted that the edge of the deck is no longer at a right angle to the face of the deck. The cards on the top of the bend appear shorter than those on the bottom. This is a result of the curve being a larger diameter on the outside than the inside of the bend. The top cards would actually have to become longer to span the distance and maintain square ends on the deck. Not only does each card in the deck bend when pressure is placed on the ends, but the cards slide or shear in relation to each other as each adjusts its position to its own diameter curve. The three forces expressed here are compression, shear, and bending.

Now imagine that glue is sandwiched between each card in a flat deck and the deck is clamped together until the glue is set. In the hand the deck has become solid; no longer can finger and thumb bend it. If the deck is placed in a vise and coaxed into a bend, its failure will eventually occur by a tearing apart of the cards. If the glue is strong, the ends of the deck will remain fairly square. An examination of the broken deck will reveal that the cards on the outside of the

curve have actually been pulled apart while those on the inside have been crumpled together. The glue did not allow the cards to slide against each other, therefore causing half the cards to be placed in tension and the other half in compression as the former tried to become longer to enclose the larger curve and the latter tried to become shorter as they were compressed into the smaller curve. In this situation there are four forces in operation: compression, bending, and resistance to shear, which causes tension. The soft bendable deck of cards became a coherent structure when glued, many times stronger than before. The glue has no structural qualities of its own, but was able to impart strength through its bonding ability. The paper from which the cards are made can easily be bent, but not so easily made longer or shorter. The 52 cards in the loose deck show only a slight resistance to the force of thumb and finger. That resistance was greatly increased with the transformation to tension and compression systems when the cards were glued together: this combined resistance was greater than the sum of the resistance of all the parts.

In structural concerns, torsion is the least prevalent, but it is the most complex, for it is a result of all four of the other forces. Torsion is twist. The practice of mechanics rests largely upon torsion; the automobile driver's hands turn the steering wheel, exerting a torsional force which is transferred torsionally to the wheels. The car might be torsionally suspended with the springing twist of a steel bar, and it is securely held together with nuts and bolts twisted into place. Torsion is actually a specialized bending, a circular bending: cantilevered beams, tree limbs, insect legs, animal bones—all have torsional forces set and resolved.

2-9 This drawing might help to give a glimpse of the balance and interplay of forces taking place within a complex form supporting only its own weight. An arch of compression spans the central beam from leg to leg. Compression is also found in the underside of the cantilevered beam. This compression is met by shear, torsion, and tension at its intersection. It can be seen that to be strong a homogeneous form such as this must be made of a material capable of resisting all those forces. This is why large structures (like the Forth Bridge) must be analyzed for force distribution and the members made accordingly.

2-10 Shearing forces are present in the motion of a paper cutter as the blade separates the fibers of paper in a squeezing, sliding, slicing, stretching action; these are the same forces present in the center of a structural member where tension on one side meets compression on the other side.

39

With these forces in both harmony and discord the living and the inanimate face the perils of existence. Among the most demanding structural needs successfully met is that found in the animal skeleton.

In the museums we see dry bones tied together with wire in loose assemblies propped up with piping. These skeletal arrangements outline the original form to give an approximation of the creatures' lifetime shape, but when the soft tissue, tendon, ligament, muscle and membrane are gone and the bone turns brittle, the skeleton indicates just the most remote clue to the dynamic mechanical unity of the animated life that developed it and then left it behind.

Only in view of the complete and living body can an appreciation of the incredibly complex balance of forces be gained. Consider for a moment the rhythm of force and stress through the human form even in the simplest of acts.

A person is seated in a chair. Most voluntary muscles are relaxed, one leg hangs loosely across the knee of the other. A decision is made to take a peanut from a dish on the table adjacent to the chair. Immediately the whole form is involved; dozens of muscles throughout the body receive the order to contract, one oblique and two straight muscles on each eye flex, turning the eyes to the side in unison.

Simultaneously other muscles are placing tensional force on the pelvis, scapula, rib cage, sternum and spinal column, causing them to go into compression, torsion, and shear. Biceps and triceps balance tension on opposite sides of the humerus in compression, to cantilever ulna and radius in a reach to place the hand upon the table. A whole group of muscles on the opposite side of the body has gone into tension against the compression of the spinal column to counterbalance the cantilevered arm.

Meanwhile, the leg has uncrossed and set foot upon the floor to stabilize the body weight. Tibia and fibula torsionally rotate the foot, then go into compression as the femur pushes down on them in a shearing stress. The flexor digitorium superficialis muscle of the lower arm draws tight and four fingers encircle the peanut, phalanges in compression and shear, tendons in tension. The arm folds back up to the mouth with the peanut in a flowing series of stresses and movement. The mouth opens when the maxillary and mandible bones separate to accept the morsel; in a crunch of compression the peanut is squashed between two molars.

Despite the impressive abilities of the human body, it is not as finely designed for structure and economy as the bodies of birds of flight. These creatures have

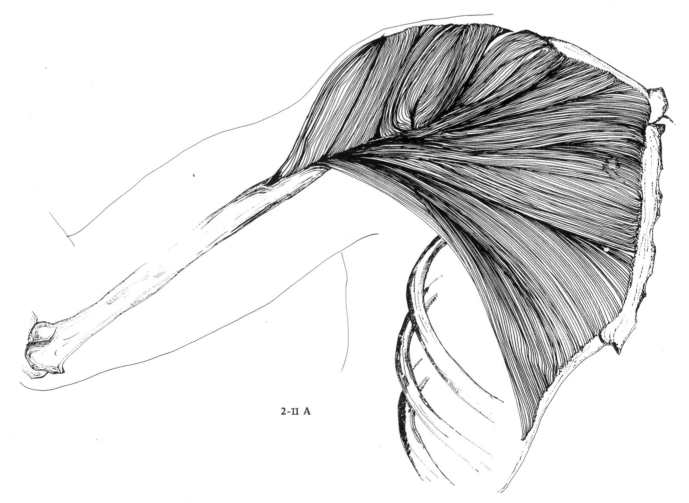

2-11 A

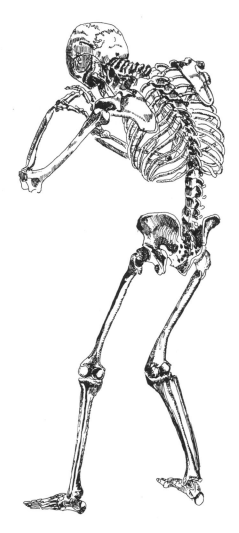

2-11 B

2-11 C

2-11 A, B, C. D.   The structure of the human body comprises two complete but interdependent systems, the materials of which are marvelously adapted to their tasks. On the inside are the semi-rigid "struts," the bones. The foundation for this system is the pelvis, which is actually four bones. The pelvis is the basin from which the twenty-six short heavy cylinders of the vertebral column spring, an assembly of bones that can be a rigid post or a flexible shaft. The ribs branch from the upper half of this column; the bones that comprise the shoulders and arms float at the top and sides of the rib cage, held in place by the tensional system. Like a finial the cranium sits atop the vertebral column. Weight is transferred from the upper body through the column to the pelvis. The pelvis divides the load to the long bones of the lower extremities.

The "ties" are the second system, a tensional network of the muscles and ligaments. Though they hold together and articulate the compressive system, muscles can't push. But with groups of muscles anchored to non-moving bones and surrounding an articulated bone, the bone, or limb may be moved in almost any direction by the coordinated contractions of sets of muscles.

In engineering terms one can be inspired by the creation of a structure that not only stays intact but is in constant dynamic equilibrium, as the body moves about. Drawing #2-11B, 2-11C after Vesalius.

2-11 D

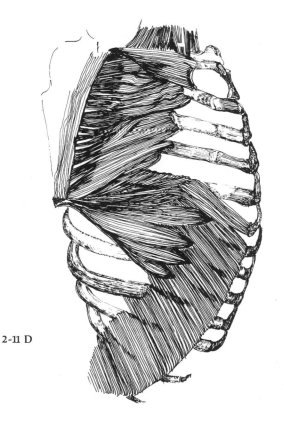

41

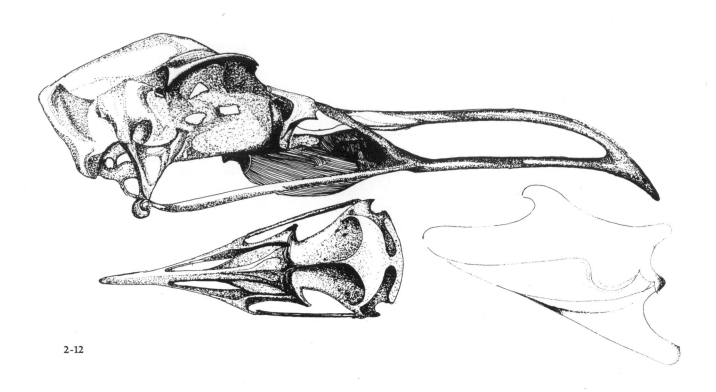

2-12

re-adapted the skeleton into a frame of exceptional strength with minimal material. All the long bones are hollow tubes instead of the solid and marrow filled bones of the land bound animals. The tube is as strong as the rod, but with a fraction of the weight. Some of these hollow bones are even used as part of the breathing and air storage apparatus of the bird.

The bird's central body bones, rib sections, backbone and sternum have fused together into a thin light shell used as a cuirass to protect the vitals and as a central anchorage for muscles. The central shell is almost transparent in its thinness but has a small bead of reinforced bone to strengthen the edges. The sternum, a less significant bone in the center of the human chest used to tie the ribcage together, has developed in the bird into a boatlike hull with a long protruding keel. This keel is used as a deep leverage point for the flight muscles of the bird. The flight muscles are centered in the body, attached to each side of the keel; they connect and operate the wings with long tendons. Pulling on these tendons positions the wing bones and feathers. With this method the wings are remotely controlled with the weight of the muscle centered in the body for stability.

The metacarpal bones in the human are the five thin ones that form the structure of the palm of the hand. They serve as foundations for the fingers. In the bird some of these bones have fused, others have

2-12 Pictured is a seagull's skull with its finely designed light and strong structure. In the lower right of the drawing is the bird's breast plate; the protuberance below is the "keel," which serves as the anchor for the flight muscles.

become shorter, and still others have elongated to form the wing tip. The metacarpals in the bird must be extremely light because they lie so far out on the wing, but they also receive great stress and so must be exceptionally strong. In the larger gliding birds like the eagle and vulture the hollow interior of the metacarpal has evolved a triangulate mesh very closely resembling steel truss bridge construction and offering the strength and lightness of the triangle.

Natural structure changes slowly from mutation to mutation over enormous periods of time. Each area of musculature, bone, and ligament alters slightly from generation to generation. As it responds to the demands of life, increasing strength here, diminishing it there, lengthening, shortening and lightening, the results are organisms with individually tailored parts, each attuned to its immediate needs. (12)

It is not yet feasible and practical with the technology and research now available to man to build structures with the principles and practices employed by nature, that of reducing the amount of material to adjust it to correspond exactly with the load, at any given point in the structure. The natural structures, such as that of the human or bird, may

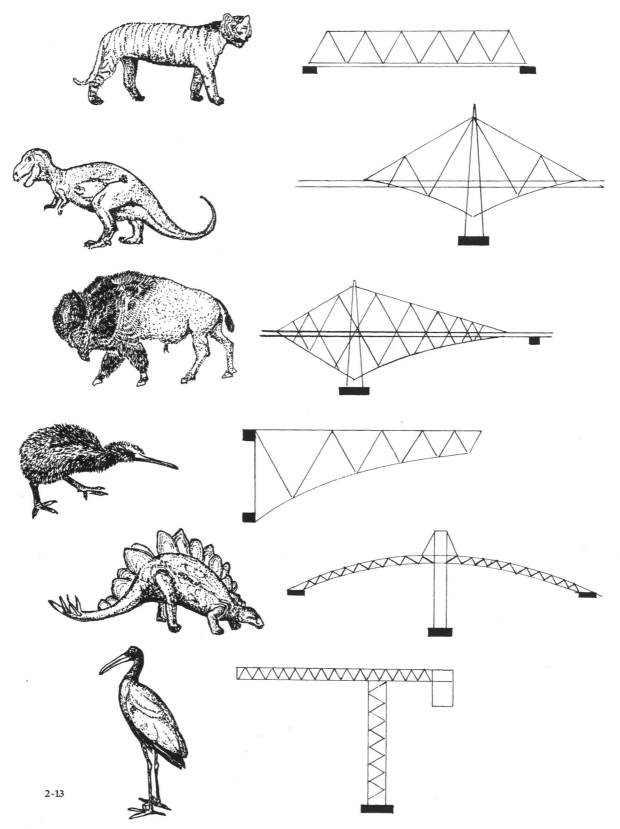

2-13

2-13 There are some interesting similarities between the animal world and the forms people create. At the top is the tiger and the Warren truss, a straight beam supported equally at each end. The tyrannosaurus is a double cantilever, a central tower supported opposing sections. The bison is an arch and a cantilever. The majority of weight comes on the forelegs; the massive cantilevered head does not quite balance the hindquarter, the weight of which is taken by the back legs. The elephant bird is a simple cantilever supported only from one end. The stegosaurus is a supported arch, half the weight taken equally at the ends, and the other half supported by a central column. The grebe is a counterbalanced crane and tower.

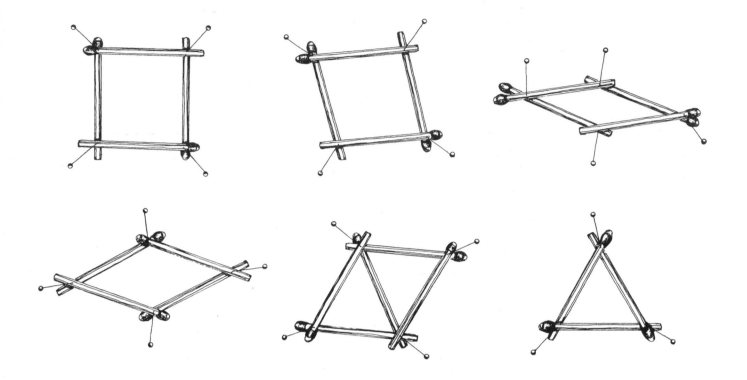

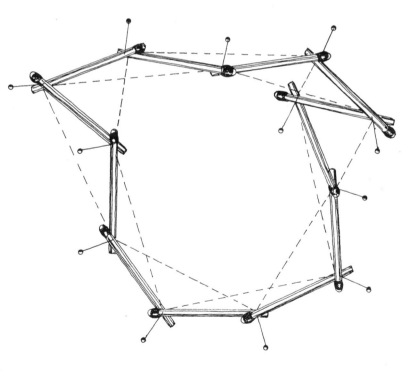

2-14 Any given form can be triangulated by connecting every third consecutive point.

not be the most successful in their present form, but by natural selection they are probably moving toward that perfect structure.

Because of this lack of technical sophistication and specialization man-made structures depend upon a generalization of form: circles and domes, squares, rectangles and triangles. They are often efficient and even economical but probably not the optimal form for a specific condition. Of these structural forms one simple shape, the triangle, is seen to be repeated over and over again in nature as well as in man-made structures. The reason for its success as a structural form is as simple as the form itself: it is intrinsically stable.

As a demonstration of the comparative abilities of the triangle and square, presume a square is formed from match sticks, the corners connected with straight pins in such a way that the pins hold the sides together but allow them to pivot. The square can be deformed to any degree desired. The square is not stable. Only by adding another member or reinforcing the corners can it be made rigid. A diagonal brace across the square actually turns it into two triangles. If a triangle is connected by pins as the square was it will not deform if the legs do not bend or break and the intersections remain intact.

This ability of the triangle is one of the basics of structure and because of this ability, the triangle is the basis for most structural forms.

When rectilinear structures such as houses are built, they must have some kind of cross-bracing to give them strength against lateral forces. These diagonals turn the rectangular side into triangles.

Structural members are usually weakest at their intersections. Due to the fact that distance increased leverage, a small force directed on the outside end of the beam places enormous forces at the intersection. Relying upon reinforced intersections for stability is structurally unsound. A far more successful joining of members can be effected by the employment of angle bracing at a distance from the intersection, thereby gaining a more favorable leverage by the use of triangulation.

Using the elegant triangle as bracing is rather like using a race horse as transportation; it works well, but its potential can never be realized within that context. The most sophisticated of man-made structures arise when the triangle is used in its pure form with structures constructed only from the triangle and its associated shapes. The simplest of these trusses result from connected triangles in one plane. Many variations of these are found in steel truss bridges. This kind of structure is very light and strong and responds well to the needs of a bridge, but is a two-dimensional solution. The triangles that comprise the structure are in flat rows to form a box in cross section. Through the center of the box or on its top, the cars and trains move.

2-15 The old timber barns of North America reflected some innate understanding of structure by their builders. The large hand-cut timbers were cross-braced to form a series of triangles which rigidified the building from lateral movement.

2-16 A and B. The Warren truss is one of the family of in-line triangulated trusses used so frequently for small bridge construction. The sides give vertical stability; the top horizontal members prevent deflection; and the roadway lies on girders crossing beneath it.

Compare this form to the accompanying drawing of the cross-section of a vulture metacarpal bone. The metacarpal is far out on the wing and so it must be as light as possible, but it also takes great stress and so must be extremely strong. Through countless generations the triangulated truss evolved in the center of the metacarpal as reinforcement, nature's solution to the same problem.

2-17 A and B. These two drawings show the same kind of reinforcing used in nature. Drawing #2-17A is looking down from the end of a crow's wing bone with its random triangulation, and 2-17B is a section of a sand dollar showing the buttressing.

2-16 A

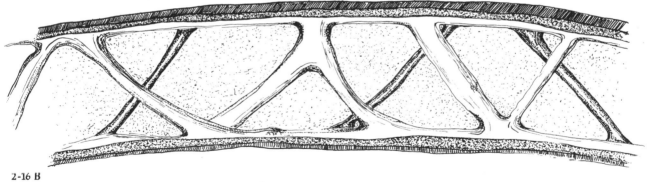

2-16 B

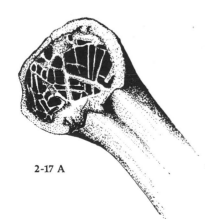

2-17 A

2-17 B

47

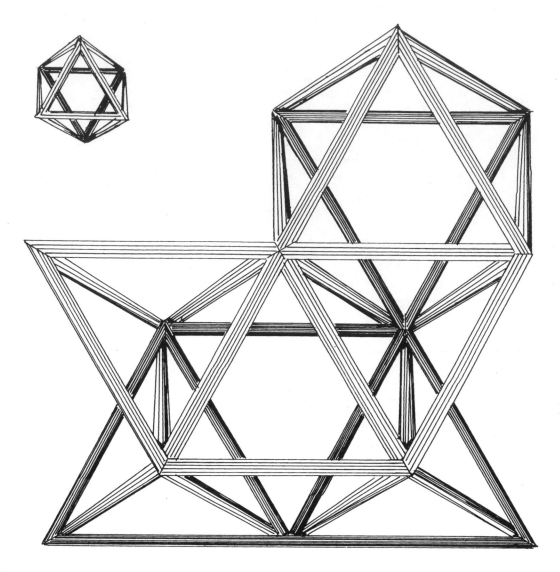

2-18

2-19

48

Hybrid structures come about through the rotation and connection of the triangle in three-dimensional space. Primarily there are three three-dimensional stable structures. The simplest is formed from four equilateral triangles placed edge to edge to comprise a three-sided pyramid, the tetrahedron. The tetrahedron with its six legs is a stable three-dimensional structure of the very least number of members possible. The next, more complex, stable structure is the octahedron, an eight-sided figure made of two square based pyramids placed together, base to base. The third is the icosahedron, a twenty-sided figure made from the intersection of four pentagons, each composed of five equilateral triangles.

There is a large number of highly sophisticated structures employing one or more of these primary forms. One family of these structures is called space grids or space frames—the space grid is used to span large distances with minimum weight. Space grids are formed with flat parallel planes comprising upper and lower surfaces, with triangulation between. One example of such a structure is formed by connecting octagons to make the octetruss, thought by many to be the strongest triangulated structure built by man. Space grids are used in the construction of roofs, walls, bridges, towers and whole buildings. (13)

The triangle-based forms discussed previously have been flat and angular. There is another family of recently popular curved forms, domes, derived from the sphere. The sphere is the most uniformly structural shape possible for resisting a load from any possible direction. To investigate some of the reasons for this quality a look at a stone wall can help.

2-18 This is a section of an octet-truss. The basic unit is to the top left in this drawing. It consists of eight equilateral triangles. These units put together can form an endless space lattice. The top and bottom patterns are a series of hexagons, in turn made of equilateral triangles. Following a straight line through the truss from the side view it would look like a Warren truss slightly slanted. The octet units can be added to the top and bottom of an existing assembly; in other words an octet-truss can completely fill any three-dimensional space. Some say that the octet-truss has the most superior strength/weight ratio of any known compression structure.

2-19 When the properties of the triangle and arch are combined, great strengths can be achieved. Most arch bridges rely on the banks of the river they span to hold the compression arch in place, the ends of the arch pushing down and out. This is not so with the hinged arch. The hinged arch is used when the arch must spring from a point in the middle of a wide river. The Bayonne Bridge spanning the Kill Van Kul River is a two-hinged arch. It is an independently strong arch; the cement piers that support its ends receive no outward thrust. The roadway hangs from the arch.

In dry stone construction no mortar is used, so the only means for the wall holding together is the friction and compression between the blocks. The stones are stacked on top of one another in a pure compression structure. If each block of stone were first chiseled into a wedge shape, then stacked, instead of rising straight, the wall would circle into an arch or vault curving back to the ground again. A stone arch might be placed between two banks of a stream as a bridge. Over the arch a roadway could be laid. The weight of the road would be carried down by pillars to rest uniformly upon the arch. The arch is the ideal structure for this kind of support. Like the dry stone wall, the arch employs no means of staying together other than the fact that the blocks are pushed surface to surface. The arch cannot collapse with a uniform load if the stone does not crumble and the banks of the stream do not move apart. As is the wall, the arch is compression formed and held intact by compression. The banks and the river bed are in tension holding the ends of the arch together.

If an infinite number of arches were rotated about a central axis placed at the center of the top of the arch, a dome would be formed. Or more simply, if a dome is sliced in half through the center, the cross section is an arch. A stone dome has the exact same structural qualities as an arch and also the stone wall. The stones are held together in compression; if the stone sphere were to have pressure from the outside released it would fall apart, as would the stone wall if gravity were to cease its pull.

In the reverse, if the materials of a sphere are switched from stone to, let us say, rubber sheeting, and the load is switched to the inside, the sphere becomes a purely tensional structure like an inflated rubber balloon. The arch, dome and sphere are powerful resistors of compression and tensional forces if the load is evenly distributed, but are very poor if the load is concentrated at one point only. This becomes the job of the truss. (14)

Very exciting possibilities arise when the structural potential of the dome is joined with the rigidity of the triangle. The dome is one of the best ways to enclose large spaces, for it resists the pull of gravity evenly over its surface, and gives stability with minimum material.

One of the families of domes is the geodesic dome. Not all triangulated domes are geodesic. A geodesic is defined as the shortest distance between two points on the surface of a solid; the earth's equator is a geodesic line; or in another way, a curve drawn upon

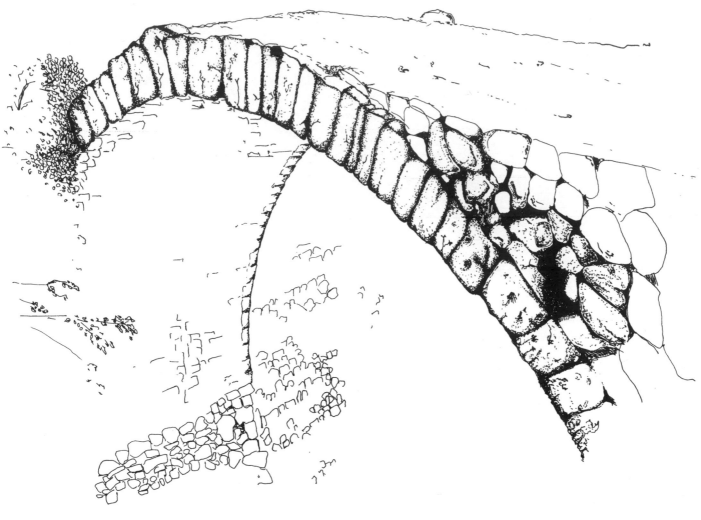

2-20

2-21

a surface so that if we take any two adjacent points on the curve, the curve gives the shortest distance between them. An airplane flying the most direct path between New York City and London is flying along a geodesic line of the earth. A geodesic dome is composed of triangles and triangle derived forms whose legs fall together to form a series of geodesic lines over the surface of the dome.

Most of this discussion has centered upon compression structures, those structures with the majority of their members in compression. Tension or tensile structures, ranging from camping tents to great bridges, are, as pointed out earlier, far stronger in a strength-to-weight ratio than are compression structures. The most complex of these tensile structures are what Buckminster Fuller has termed "tensegrity." His approach results in some of the best strength-weight ratios yet achieved, because there is the smallest number of compression parts, which are usually the heaviest members. Compression structures, Fuller has pointed out, are structured with a continuous connection of compression members throughout the structure, and the tension members are discontinuous, or islands in the compression. Common tension structures, though they may have a majority of their members in tension, still have continuous compression and discontinuous tension. In tensegrity structures (integrity + tension), the compression is isolated and floated in a continuous field of tension. The future of tensegrity structures is hard to judge, for they are difficult to erect, temperamental to use, and require exacting use of materials. (15)

In addition to Fuller there have been a few other remarkable people who have dealt with structure. Robert Maillart and Pier Nervi are among those who worked with compression structures in concrete, and Frei Otto has worked with the tensile structure of inflatables and large scale tents. Many of Otto's ideas came directly from nature, as did Fuller's. Otto found direction from such things as the glass skeletons of minute diatoms on the sea floor, tree symmetry, and mammalian vertebrae, turning these forms into

structures for man's use. He has examined the possibilities of creating a massive backbone of steel casings and wire to be used as a crane. Wire members on one side, acting as muscle and tendon, would relax their tension, allowing the crane to dip in the opposite direction. When the wire tension members tightened, the backbone would straighten, lifting the object and swinging it at any location within a radius of the crane.

The development of human technology in structure is well followed and well documented from the past to the present. The first man-made structures were piles of loose stone and wood which rose vertically and horizontally. Structure was at a minimum. The Greeks used the simplest of structures. They did not have the arch, and thus could span roofs only with many columns topped with short, heavy, horizontal lintels. The Romans discovered and developed the arch, which allowed them to cover huge areas with vaults and domes without a forest of pillars. With the arch and the dome, structures appeared that were stronger and lighter. The Gothic builders set stone upon stone to heights never before nor since achieved in that material without reinforcement. The next structural changes came from the material itself as cast iron replaced stone and wood, wrought iron replaced cast iron and structural steel replaced them all. With steel, long, thin trusses could be made. Steel cable and rod could be rolled and woven to stiffen pre-stressed concrete. With steel, skyscrapers and suspension bridges were possible. (16)

The methods of Fuller and Otto represent the near future. The slightly more distant future might see the development of quite different approaches to structure. The new structural technology will undoubtedly rely upon an assortment of new materials that are made for specialized tasks. The progress of man's understanding traces a movement from crude overbuilding and understructuring to economy of materials and specialization of members to the forces of tension, compression, shear and torsion.

Structure and materials are so interdependent they cannot be regarded individually, but magnitude controls them both.

2-20 This ancient Roman bridge in central northern Italy has stood all these years with no mortar to bind the stones together. The stone blocks are locked firmly into place by their fit and the constant pull of gravity holding them in position between the banks they span.

2-21 Above is a steel tube (compression) and steel wire (tension) dome. It consists of two shells of hexagons separated with a space between. It is not a geodesic dome (see text). This dome outside Cleveland, Ohio was designed by Buckminster Fuller.

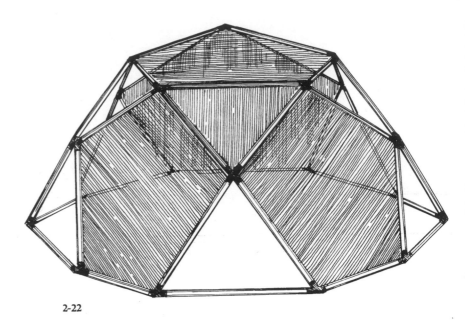

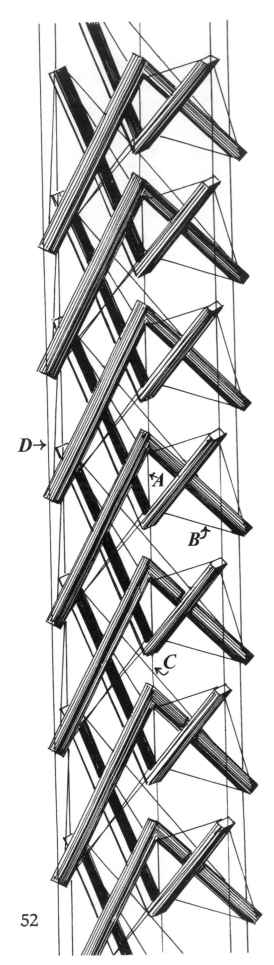

2-22 This is a small geodesic dome made up of pentagons and equilateral triangles. The geodesics are the straight lines that encircle the dome's surface.

2-23 This tower is one of a family of tension structures that has been termed tensegrity by Buckminster Fuller. In most compression and tension structures the compression is a continuous element connected throughout the structure. Every compression member is connected to the rest; the tension members are isolated. The principal of tensegrity (tension + integrity) is that the tension is continuous and the compression is isolated and discontinuous. Tensegrity structures can take many forms: towers (as pictured), space grids, and domes. Tensegrity structures are extremely light and strong. They are light because the bulky compression members are minimal, and they are strong because of the unique qualities of tension structure (see text and drawing 2-8). In addition to this, the tensegrity structure has the ability to distribute the load throughout its entire form; thus no one point is overloaded.

In the tower pictured here two opposing "V" forms are held together by the short line between the inside of the apexes (A). Opposite are the lines connecting the outside points of the "V's" (B). Each pair of opposing "V's" is held to the next pair by the short line between their points (C) and opposed by the four long lines running up the sides (D).

2-24 Robert Maillart has been noted for his elegant use of arch-supported concrete bridges, most of them erected over the rivers and gorges of Switzerland. They express an understanding of form, material, and structure. Pictured is a hinged arch cement bridge over the River Thur. Note the lack of abutment, for the hinged arch is self-contained.

2-25 As man-made structures become more sophisticated the strength is found in different ways. Early buildings were not only very heavy but rigid, they broke but did not bend. The modern concept is strength gained through flexibility, while retaining exceptional lightness; this is the concept of elastic stability.

The elastic structure is able to absorb high stress at concentrated points and distribute it, resist rapid impact and shock, bridge areas of damage and generally spread the load to the total structure thereby gaining resiliency.

An example of this kind of strength can be seen in the comparison between the rigidity of the tin can, which deforms under an excess load, and the flexible woven basket which springs back when the load is removed.

D→

A

B

C

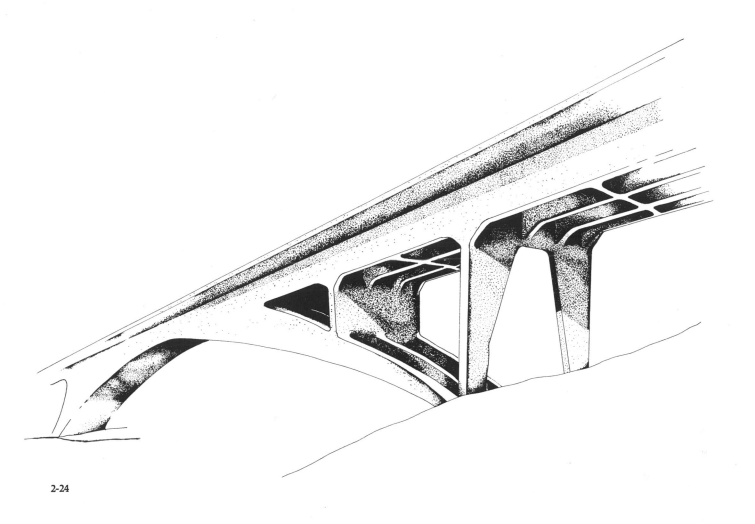

2-24

2-25

53

3 | SIZE

"Were the force of gravity to be doubled, our bipedal form would be a failure. The majority of terrestrial animals would resemble snakes. Birds would suffer likewise. But, insects would suffer less and some of the smaller would hardly change; microbes would undergo no hardship nor change. On the other hand, if gravity were halved, we should get a lighter, slender, more active form, need less energy, less heat, less lungs, and less blood and muscle." But the microbes would not profit one bit." (17)

The massive old oak caught by a late spring storm of heavy wet snow shatters beneath the excess of weight, but the five-inch sapling bends double and snaps back into place as the snow melts. The big things are less successful in holding themselves together than the small, and the bigger they are the more difficulty they have in structuring themselves against the forces they encounter. It is impossible to speak of structure and materials without considering relative magnitude.

There are huge cats and little rhinos, big puddles and small oceans. Scale is relative, and our personal experience and environment determine our concept of size. The chair is far away from the table, but it is a short trip from here to Buffalo. From floor level a child's parents are enormous but, out of the window of a lifting-off airplane, they shrink to ant-size, then dots. The butterfly is gross and overbearing to the mosquito, which is a monstrosity to the ameoba.

But scale, or magnitude, is also absolute. There are certain undeniable partitions that divide both the living and non-living into worlds apart as their magnitude changes. Although our instruments and eyes carry us into minute particles of matter and to the scope of our universe, there are worlds denied to our bodies, which are locked into a relatively narrow range of scale which has determined their form and imposed a prison. The science fiction movies, and even some early entomologists, have taken great pleasure in speculating on a train-sized ant and a building-sized beetle, which, proportionately, increase their power to knock cities apart. But such can never be, for not only would the insect's power diminish to that of scarcely being capable of lifting its own antennae, but its legs would shatter under the bulk. Probably its hollow-framed exoskeleton would burst, for the insect was designed only for its scale. Such are the principles of similitude or dynamic similarity.

3-1 The form of the oak tree is a result of its genetic makeup, but other physical laws modify those genetic commands. The limitations of size also help determine the height of the crown, spread of limbs, and girth of trunk. Most forms are a result of mutual control from a large number of sources.

3-2 The light, thin proportions of the mosquito are only possible at small sizes. Were the mosquito to double or triple in size, its form would have to become much heavier. The legs would become shorter, and its mechanism of flight would have to change.

3-1

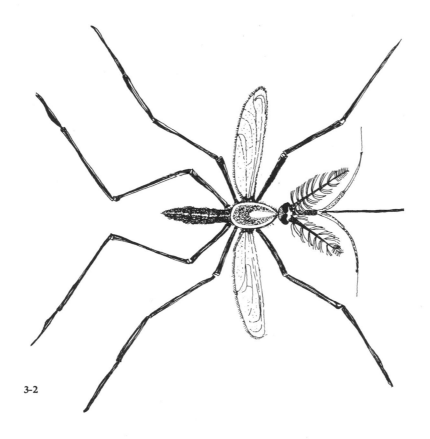

3-2

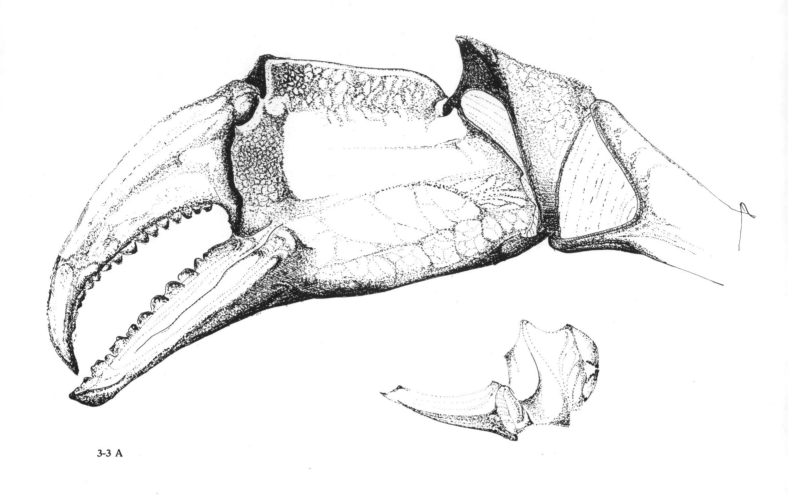

3-3 A

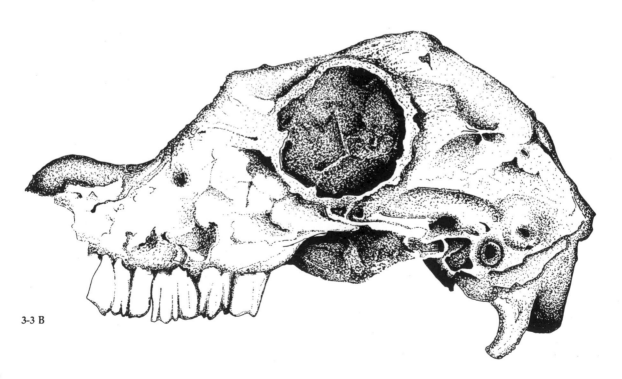

3-3 B

56

Of the gravitational forces at work in any object, some vary in response to one power and some to another, and the relative values of these forces alter with scale. The strength of a wooden beam varies with the size of its cross section, and all the cross sections vary to the square of their linear dimensions, but the weight of the total beam varies as to the cube of its linear dimensions; in other words, it becomes disproportionately heavy as it grows larger. This is called the law of dynamic similarity.

A granite pebble will bounce on a stone floor with only a slight mar to its surface even if let fall from a great height, but, to split a granite boulder, it need be dropped only a distance a few times its diameter. A mountain of granite would crumble were the ground beneath it to shift slightly. A toothpick can be held between finger and thumb in a horizontal position with no apparent sagging, but a log 100 feet in length and of the same proportion would bend to the breaking point if supported at both ends.

A small tree trunk can serve adequately well as a foot bridge across a stream, but a larger river one quarter of a mile wide would require a more careful consideration of form and structure to span its bank; a mammoth trunk would serve very poorly. This same phenomenon holds in other materials; if a solid steel sewing needle the size of a large redwood tree were thrust point down into a mammoth pincushion, it would bend to the ground like soft wax of its own weight, a problem that the redwood escapes with its lesser weight and its size-structured proportions.

3-3 A and B. Nature successfully uses the exoskeleton with the smaller creatures. Insects usually have their structures on the outside like the ant and the beetle. The exoskeleton is a semi-rigid hollow vessel containing the soft tissue within. The exoskeleton is succesful in animals up to the size of a crab. Large turtles' shells must be very thick and so become a great burden to the animal, past practical limits. Even the crab and lobster are in some jeopardy with their larger body plates, for they are easily broken. The crab claw is sectioned for greater strength as well as flexibility.

Hollow forms become considerably weaker as size increases (see text). The small tin can is quite strong, but the proportionately heavier metal garbage can dents easily. For the larger animals nature uses the interior skeleton to better accommodate weight distribution. The only hollow form used in larger animals is the skull, like the sheep's skull shown.

3-4 Without our really being conscious of it, the proportions of similar things of different size very tremendously. On the right are three trees drawn accurately in scale; they appear logically proportioned. On the left the three trees are shown in their own proportion but at the same size. The sequoia (far left) looks awkward and stubby, while the Norway spruce looks spindly, and only the Douglas fir (center) seems to be in scale.

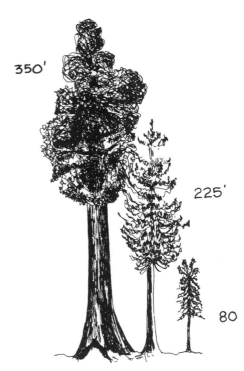

350'

225'

80

3-4

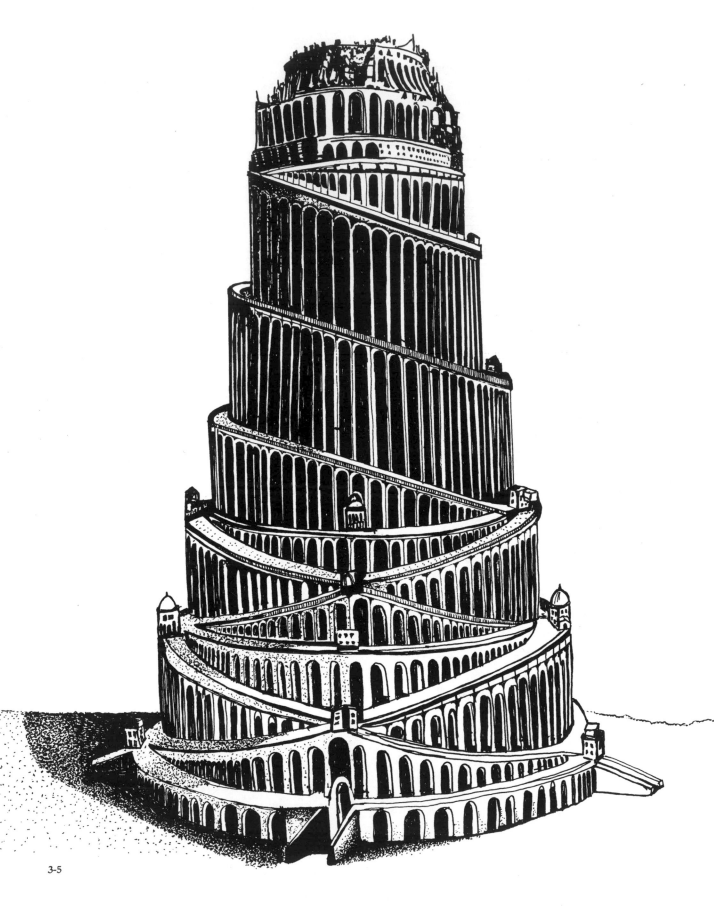

3-5

Galileo, who discovered the laws of dynamic similarity, saw that they governed the form of all things on this earth. Since he was a mechanical consultant and an inquisitive man, Galileo often wandered through the Venetian arsenal and dockyard observing the massive operation of shipbuilding.

"At times," he wrote, "I have been put to confusion and driven to despair of ever explaining something for which I could not account, but which my senses told me to be true ... why they employ stocks, scaffolding, and bracing of larger dimensions for launching a big vessel than they do for a small one."

An old artisan of the dockyard told him that it has been discovered that it was necessary "to avoid the danger of the ship parting under its own heavy weight, a danger to which smaller boats were not subject."

After investigation and demonstrations, Galileo concluded that "the larger machine, built of the same material and in the same proportion as the smaller, corresponding with exactness to the smaller in every respect ... will not be so strong or so resistant against violent treatment; the larger the machine, the greater its weakness."

Galileo realized that the principles of dynamic similarity also apply to the natural sciences. He wrote: "... nor can nature produce trees of extraordinary size, because the branches would break under their own weight; so also it would be impossible to build up the bony structure of man, horses, or other animals so as to hold together and perform their normal functions if these animals were to be increased enormously in height ... To illustrate briefly, I have sketched a bone whose natural length has been increased three times and whose thickness has been multiplied until, for a correspondingly larger animal, it would perform the same function which the small bone performs for its small animal.

3-5 Building projects of enormous size have always held an intrigue for people, from the ancients onward. Some structures, like the pyramids, were constructed to insure immortality, others to commemorate, honor, acclaim, testify, defend, and many societies dreamed of constructing a building so tall that it could touch the sky, and so provide a very direct access to heaven. The tower of Babel was for such a purpose. It is not known how high it might have reached or if construction was ever even started, but according to legend it was never completed, for the heavenly beings became alarmed at the possibilities of intrusion and sent the builders "babbling" off in strange languages.

In modern times the architect Frank Lloyd Wright designed a building to be one mile high, and the sculptor, architect, and social philospher Paolo Soleri has designed structures so vast that a single free-standing building could house a city, factories, airports, and several million people.

Whether of selfish or noble purpose, attempts at structures of such magnitude are physically impaired from the onset, for strength diminishes as size increases. Gigantic sizes may not be impossible to achieve, save to the heavens, but they require such additional buttressing, reinforcing, and proportionately greater mass that levels of impracticability are reached.

3-6 This drawing was taken after one made by Galileo. He drew it to demonstrate the necessities brought about by change in size. At the bottom is a normally proportioned animal bone; at the top is a bone drawn to three times the length but increased enough in girth to have it retain its proportionate strength. It can be seen that as things increase in size (length) they must be of much greater mass.

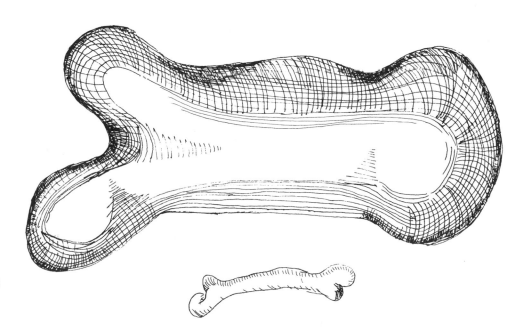

3-6

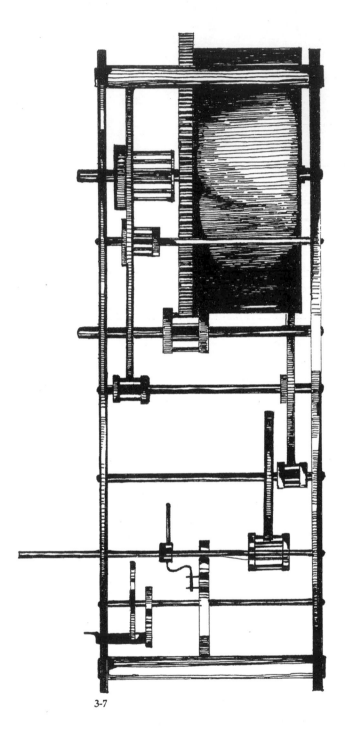

3-7

Clearly then, if one wishes to maintain in a great giant the same proportions of limb as that of an ordinary man ... he must admit a diminution of strength in comparison with men of medium stature," or the form will "suggest a monstrosity." And the reverse is also true, if the size be diminished the strength of the body will greatly increase. "Thus," as Galileo concludes, "a small dog could probably carry on his back two or three dogs of his own size; but I believe that a horse could not even carry one of his own size."

The living are locked into their own orders of magnitude by their activities, the material from which they are made, their structure and form. Berries, plums, cherries and lemons easily hang from their parent tree, apples and oranges present some problems to the tree's structure, and grapefruit strain the tree and the stem from which they hang. Melons lie upon the ground. An impractically large stem would be required to hold a healthy pumpkin safely aloft in fall weather.

As size shifts from small to large, strength dwindles, forms change, but the materials remain the same. It is an obvious, but nonetheless interesting, observation to note that the big and the small are made of the same materials. It might seem logical that big things would be made up of bigger particles of matter than the small. The granite face of a mountain might consist of tennis ball-sized molecules, giant aircraft built with metals that have great pinhead atoms. Redwood trees and whales should not contain the same sized cells that fleas and buttercups have. But such is not the case; the hippopotamus and the one-celled protozoa have cells very little different in size. Steel bridge girders and hair line escapement springs in the smallest of watches consist of essentially the same sized particles. The big things in our universe are just larger accumulations of the same bits of matter. (18)

Though the matter that builds the form does not

3-7 Though the forms of things vary greatly in size the molecules from which they are made are much the same size. The size of the molecules in the metal of a clock works, watch or the steel of a bridge or office building are approximately the same size.

3-8 A and B These microscopic forms develop completely free from the constraints of gravity but must follow the dictates of other laws.

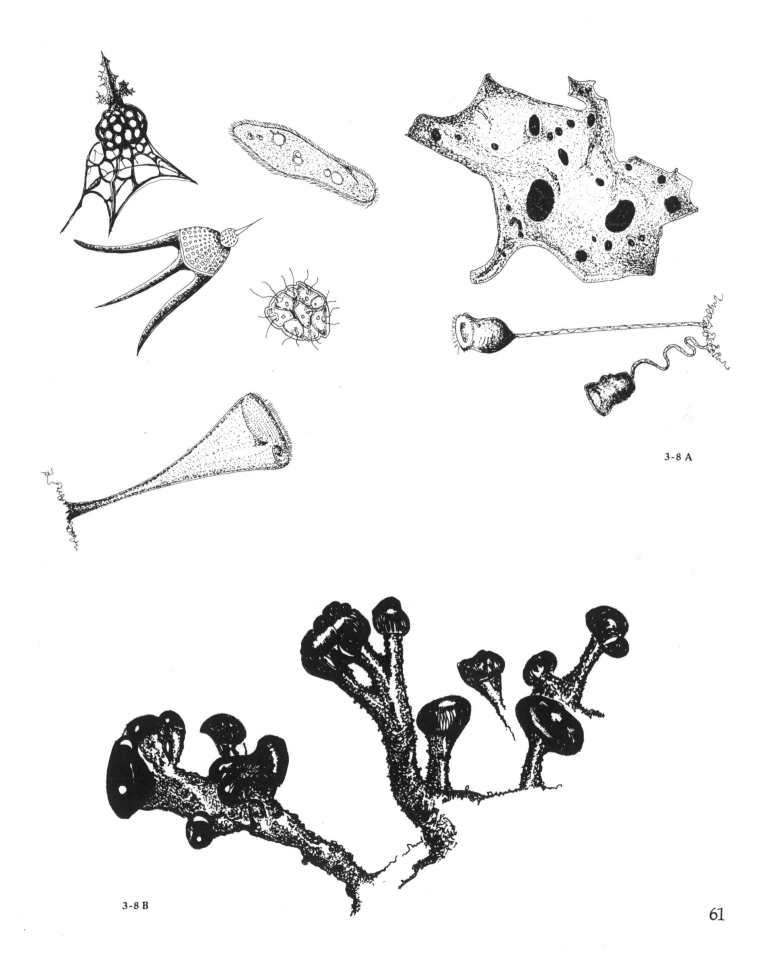

3-8 A

3-8 B

61

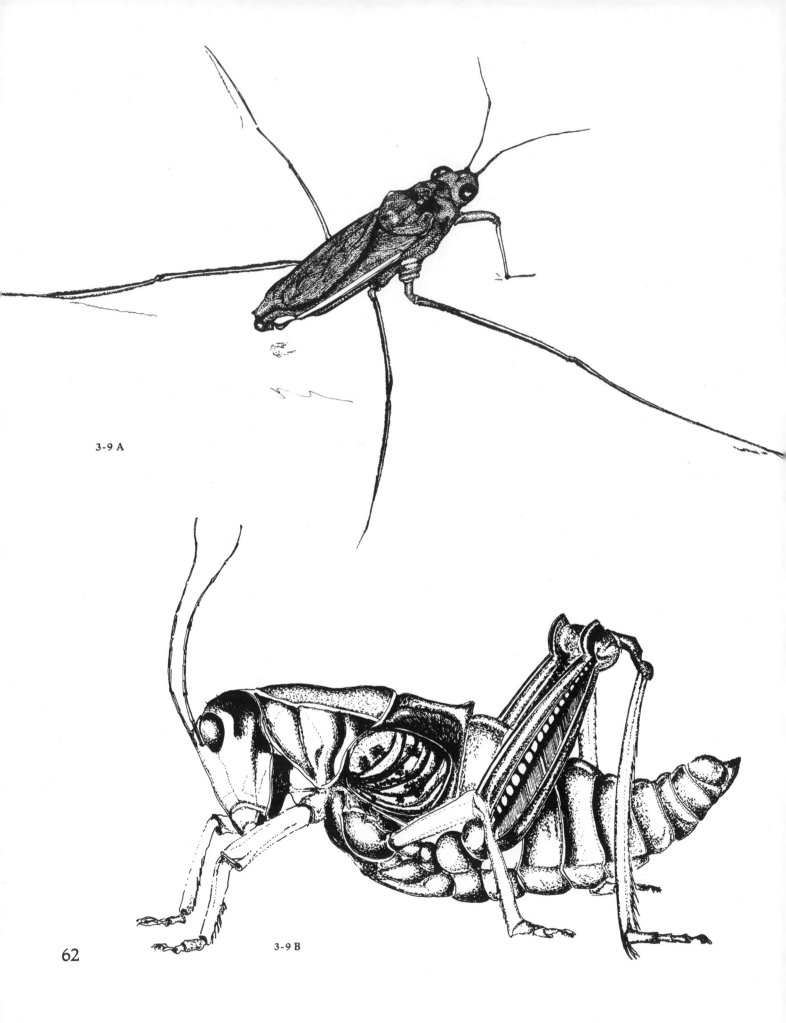

3-9 A

3-9 B

62

change with size, the forms themselves change tremendously as size shifts. This change is caused by a variety of influences at different size levels. The very small develop independent of gravity. Single-celled microbes assume shapes that respond to forces quite separate from those that influence the large multicelled animals. Molecular activity affects the smallest of these microbes. The minute bacteria at the far edge of life are almost totally free of the influence of gravity but must contend with a helter-skelter bombardment of molecules; this is called the Brownian movement. These microbes are so small that the actual movement of the molecules that make up the medium in which they exist exerts upon them an impact force that moves them about.

Microbes often develop in a watery environment and the actual viscosity of the medium in which the organism lives becomes an influential force in its development. A protozoan will have to push its way through a drop of water which is to the protozoan quite dense, and may even be approaching that of the viscosity inside its cell membrane. Slight changes in heat and the evaporation of water in which the microbe lives can cause a great rush of current which tosses the microbes about. At these slight orders of size, other forces such as minute electrical charges and chemical reactions move in to affect life activity and form.

3-9 A and B   A flea can jump up to 200 times its own length; a grasshopper can jump to 75 times its length; a frog 15 times, a rabbit 7 times; a dog 5 times; a human about 2 times; a horse usually only one time; and a hippopotamus ½ its own length. It is true that the grasshopper (as shown above) may have a superior jumping mechanism, but the size differential is more influential than any other factor.

These microbes develop almost free from the effects of gravity and so grow into forms not possible at greater sizes. The single-celled stentor resembles a tornado touched down to earth and billowing out in a funnel from a pinched point of connection. The vorticella is a cup on an extraordinarily long stem. Others are elaborate helmets of glass and cushions of needles. They roll, bounce and bump through their short lives with no up and down, no top and no bottom. Their forms would be impossible at our size level. (19)

A flea can jump up to two hundred times its own length but can become imprisoned should a leg penetrate a drop of water. At the size of a flea, the surface tension of a liquid is a force with which to be reckoned. To some, such as the whirlygig or the water skeeter, surface tension has caused a whole pattern of life to emerge. These little creatures and others like them completely depend upon that slight membrane-like surface that coats ponds and rivers. Surface tension causes the surface of such liquids as water to form "skins" that contract tensionally. These "skins" afford a slippery but firm footing for many insects; however, if the "skins" were to be momentarily pierced by an insect's leg or body they would elastically close around the entrapped appendage, making it difficult if not impossible to be withdrawn by the insect. A small insect encased in a drop of water is helpless until the water evaporates.

"Up" and "down" have relevance, though, when gravity pulls the larger creatures down. As size increases, the forms of living respond ever more to the pressures of gravity and a need for structuring becomes more apparent. The ant and beetle are

63

hollow shells supported on tensional shafts. Tubular leg sections move out from the body in a horizontal direction then joint down to the ground. Their bodies are held over space between the cantilevered leg buttresses, reflecting a difficult and deft job of creating a highly mobile structure.

The hollow skeletal container is cast aside as we look up this continuum of size. The internally-structured frame, the skeleton, is better able to cope with increasing sizes than the proportionately weakening hollow vessel. The legs move closer to a point beneath the center of gravity as the pull becomes downward. The hind leg of a cat or dog is bent for rapid movement, but the bend is within the anterior outline of the animal's frame. The joints do not come out perpendicular to the body, but lie next to it. The large lizards, like alligators, have grown too big for the perpendicularly-jointed legs, so can only move about with difficulty on land. The animals of still greater magnitude have straight legs to better act in compression as the pull of gravity increases. At the far end of this continuum are the hippopotamus and the elephant. Straight pillars of compression are their legs, set beneath the four corners of the massive body.

Those animals that chose to remain waterbound or returned to the water are able to moderate their structural problems by the absorbing and spreading qualities of the water. Consider the form of the ill-structured jelly fish and try to imagine it coping on land without the cradling of its ocean environment.

3-10 Smaller animals usually have legs that are jointed to the body in a perpendicular fashion. The legs of these animals come directly out from the torso, thus springing the body with nothing beneath. This method gives good agility. Though the small lizards are very swift, the larger reptiles with perpendicularly jointed legs are slow and awkward like the iguana shown above. More successful in creatures of this size are legs that are below the weight, as in the dog or horse.

3-11 The whale could not survive structurally on land. As large as the whale bone is, it is not massive enough to hold the tons of flesh intact as a dynamic land creature. The whale must have the buoyancy of the sea. Due to the laws of dynamic similarity (see text) the whale has the advantage of heat conservation. With its massive bulk the whale radiates proportionately less heat than do small aquatic mammals. The whale also has a proportionately easier time moving through the water than do the little creatures of the sea.

The eyes of the living develop in response to visible light waves and so change in size far less than the animals and insects that they serve. The whale eye is about one three-thousandth of the whale's overall size; the human eye is about one two-hundredth of body size, and the mosquito eye is about an eighth the size of its body.

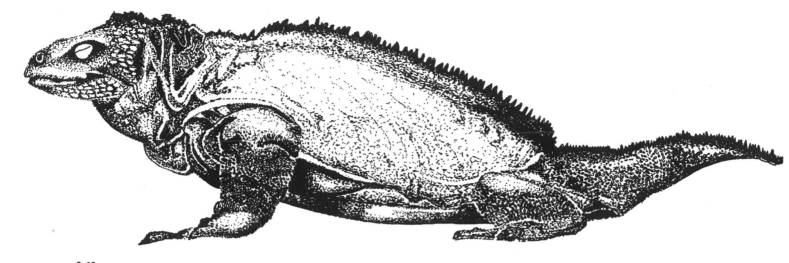

3-10

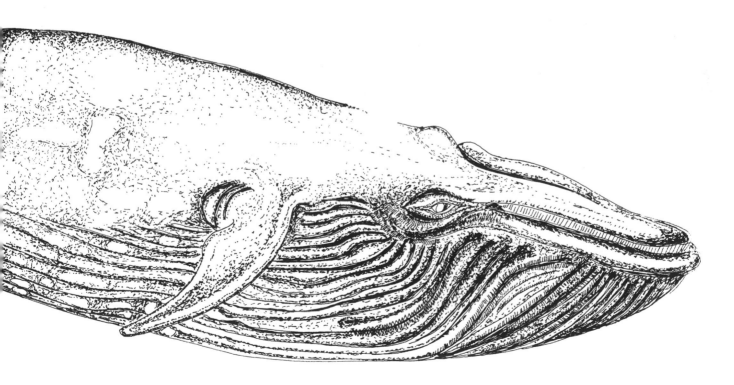

3-11

Fish skeletons and bones are thin and flexible to absorb the weight of the water and accommodate the fish's undulating movements; they are not built for the unidirectional pull of gravity. The whale would not structurally survive if its bulk were shifted to the land. It grew to its enormous size only by the buoyant help of the water.

Elephants lumber through life on the far edge of land animal size. Their thick legs are placed below them as compressive columns; their necks are short and heavy to hold a massive head. In comparison to

the elephant, consider the daddy long-legs near the other end of the scale of walking creatures. If the elephant and long-legs were reduced to a like size and viewed from an end, two rounded forms would be seen, one supported from directly beneath with legs that almost equal the mass of the body, the other hanging in space with nothing supporting it from below. The long-legs' body is held by legs that radiate up from all sides, then cantilever out and down; the spindle shanks are long, thin, and in constant tension. The long-legs, however, is agile at its magnitude only. Were it to be increased even four times in size, its form would suffer.

This range of force and influence might be regarded as points of light spaced through the orders of scale. As size grows or diminishes, the lights gradually grow brighter and slowly fade off as the next point of light intensifies its influence. The impact of molecular activity means as little to the horse as gravity means to the bacteria.

More than just determining form, size indicates a whole life pattern. Most large animals have low oxygen consumption, low energy and low food intake; they walk slowly, have a slower wing beat and movement, their voices are lower, their hearts beat more slowly, and they live longer than the small. Most small animals consume vast amounts of food for their size and have a very rapid heart rate. They have a fast walk, a fast wing beat, and their movements are rapid; they consume more oxygen proportionately, need higher energy foods, have higher voices, and they live a shorter time.

3-12 It is likely that the enormous land creatures of the past like this brachiosaurus with its head height of forty feet and ponderous body spent a good portion of their time immersed in water, for the effort of constantly coping with the force of gravity must have been much strain on the organs and muscles of their bodies. Water gave them some rest.

3-13 A, B, C. Fish like the yellow perch have a skeletal system that is structured to function without the pull of gravity. Their skeleton is designed to support the activities of the fish's life in a multidirectional manner. The land animals are structured to orient themselves against a constant one-directional pull, and so must have a weight-absorbing structural system. The jellyfish not only cannot function out of water, but will not even remain intact out of water.

3-12

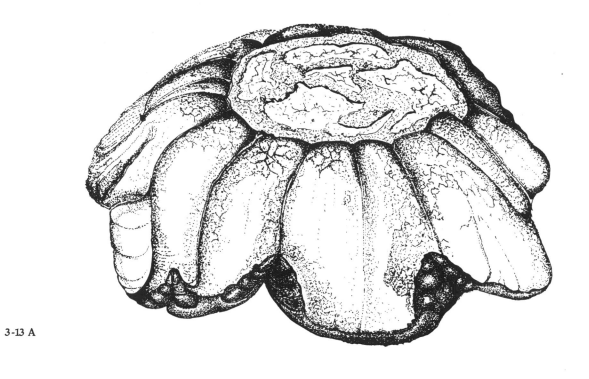

3-13 A

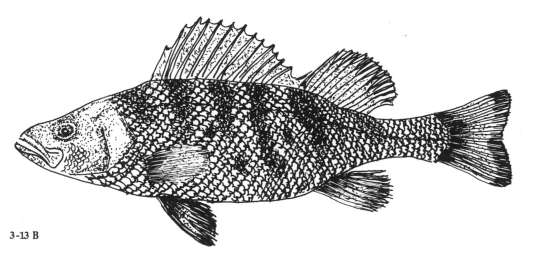

3-13 B

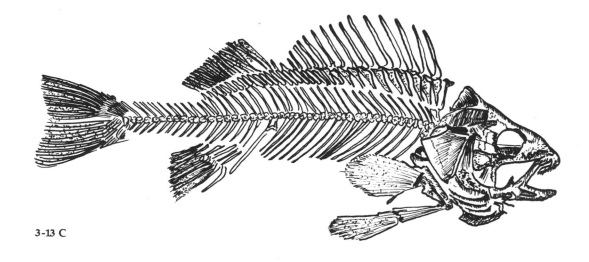

3-13 C

67

While the little springtail snaps its body in violent activity, the small spider darts from cover to cover. The little birds and the chipmunks move from place to place on the ground in a series of starts and stops. Cats and foxes are very rapid, but smoother in their movements. The tiger attains high speeds but takes longer to reach them as one motion flows into another. The horse, zebra, and elk approach the limits of graceful action. The ox is sedate and the brontosaurus was probably awkward.

3-14

3-14 The shrew and bat are the smallest mammals. The shrew is less than two inches in length and weighs about an ounce. Warm blooded creatures smaller than a shrew would probably not be possible because of the enormous quantities of food required to maintain body temperature. Because of the laws of similitude (see text) small mammals like the shrew give off proportionately more heat.

3-15 Grasping mechanisms like claws, hooks, suction cups, pincers, are needed more on small creatures to hold them in place. The bigger animals only need the friction of their weight resting on flat feet like those of the elephant.

The "rate of life" is a term that refers to the speed by which life is consumed. Most small creatures are born, mature, eat, reproduce, move and are ready for death in a fraction of the time the big animals demand, but it may not be just to speak of the big and the small together. One, it is true, may be alive two hundred times longer than the other, but the small organisms' investment in, and return from, the fraction of a minute, should not be compared to the years of life the big, like the hippopotamus, can afford to spend basking in the African sun.

D'Arcy Thompson writes that "a man will consume a fiftieth part of his own weight of food daily, but a mouse will eat its own weight in a day ..." "A warm-blooded animal much smaller than a mouse becomes an impossibility; it could neither obtain nor yet digest the food required to maintain its constant temperature, and hence no mammals and no birds are as small as the smallest frogs or fishes. The disadvantage of small size is all the greater when loss of heat is accelerated by conditions, as in the Arctic, or by convection, as in the sea. The far north is a home of large birds but not small ... and there are no small mammals in the sea." (20)

The small creatures can rush about with a fraction of the effort of the large, but they have to have more adaptations for staying in place. A fly with blunt, smooth feet like the elephant would be whisked about at the whim of every slight eddy of wind. And a mouse with human feet would have difficulty obtaining the traction needed to push off in a run without claws to hold the surface. As the creatures increase in size, their holding mechanisms are needed less, from hooks and suckers in the very small, to claws and hands in the medium range, to hooves in the larger. The flat-footed elephant needs only gravity to hold him squarely in place.

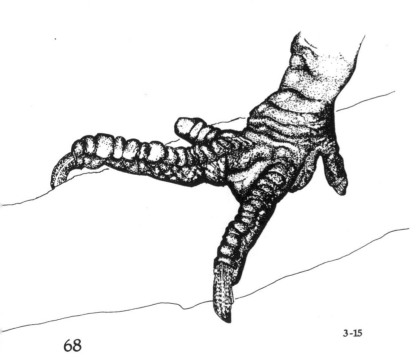

3-15

68

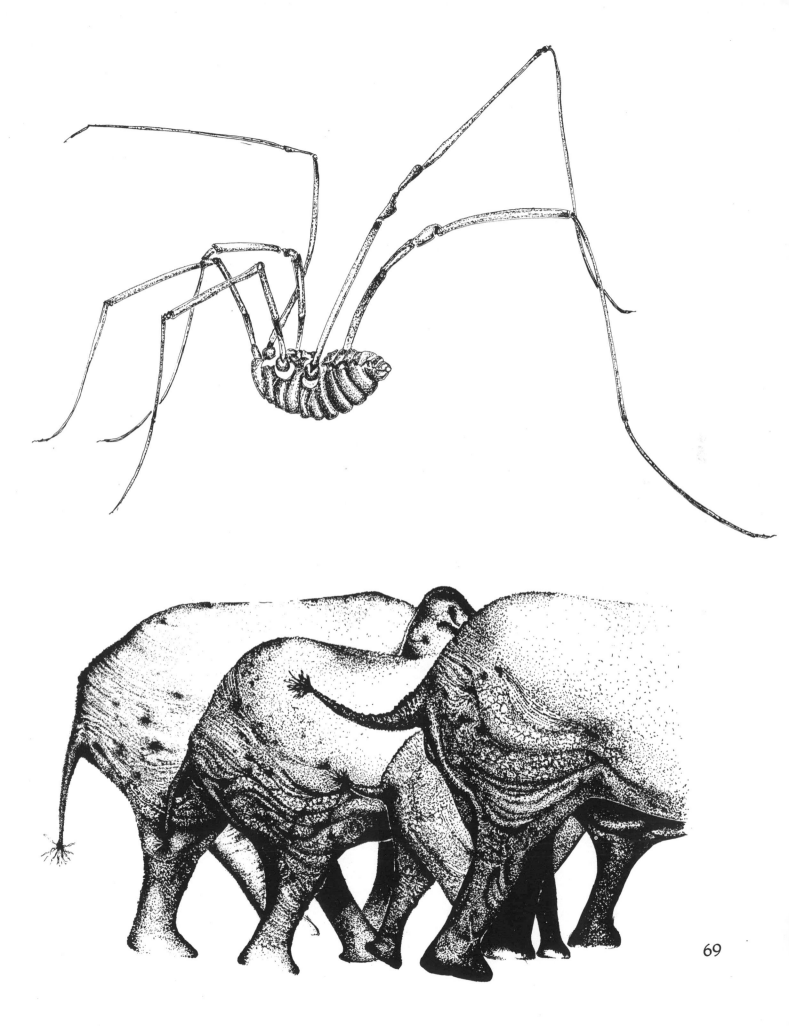

69

3-16

Although there is overlapping, the flying creatures are smaller as a group than those that walk. Among those that fly, the larger are again at a disadvantage. The work that can be done by the bird varies with available size of the muscle; that is to say, the size of the bird. The work that must be done varies with the mass and the distance; the larger the bird the greater its burden. Every time the size of the bird doubles (from a robin to a seagull, for instance), the difficulty of flight is increased at a ratio of 1 to 1.4. If we compare an ostrich to a sparrow, one being twenty-five times bigger than the other, the ostrich would have five times as hard a job flying as the sparrow. So the ostrich has surpassed the upper limits of practical flapping winged flight.

For this reason the larger birds must depend upon gliding flight to rest their muscles; the larger they are the more time must be spent in gliding. Small birds are able to dart and hover and even vertically lift off;

3-16   Larger birds often need assists to become airborne, like the seagull pushing off with its feet. Some must spring from elevated positions or slap the ground or water with wingtips before they are in the air. Larger birds are less successful flyers than are the small birds. Flying insects are still better adapted to the air.

3-17 A, B, C   With the flapping mechanism of birds and insects there is an upper limit to size, above which flight is not possible. This is because the amount of muscle to power the wings must be so great that the weight of the bird is increased to such a degree that even greater muscle is needed, which in turn hampers flight that much more, and so on. The moa bird has surpassed that limit and so is no longer capable of flight, and hence has lost its flight mechanism. The insect, though, is a magnificent flyer because of the advantage of small size.

the larger birds often need assists such as running and jumping to get off the ground. Flying insects are even better aviators, able to stop in the air without moving their bodies while their wings beat at an incredible rate of speed. If Icarus had been able to outfit himself with proportionately large wings to lift his great human frame above the ground, something more than half his body weight would be by necessity pectoral muscle. The primary flight muscle in birds, this muscle constitutes about 1/85th of man's total weight.

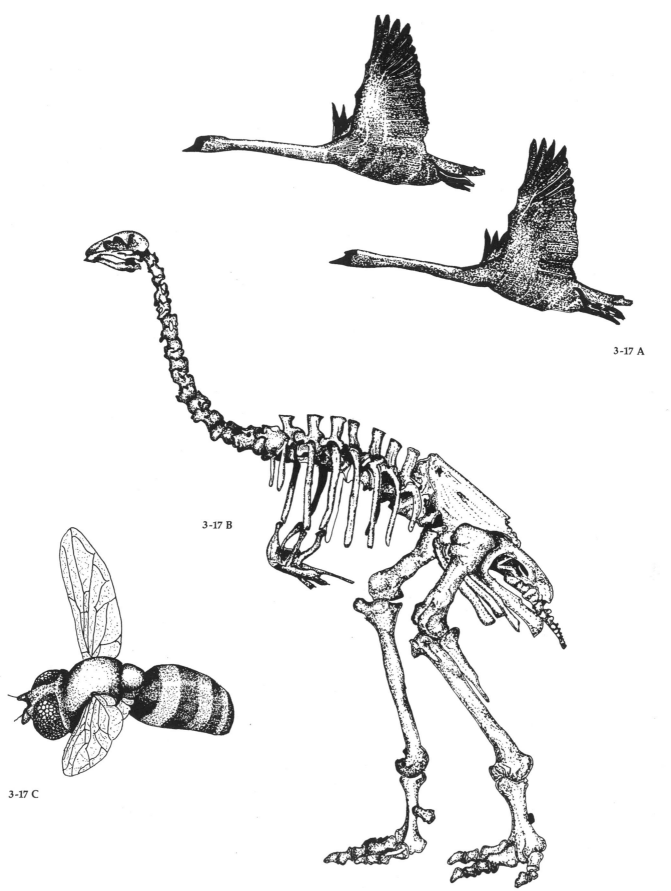

3-17 A

3-17 B

3-17 C

The effects of size can bring both great advantage and disadvantage to man. Larger office buildings need far more structure proportionately to hold them up, but they expose less surface, which means greater control of temperature and more efficiency. Super-tankers are more efficient than small ships, because of the laws of dynamic similarity. The volume, or payload, can be increased by eight times while the hull surface is only increased four times. This lesser proportion of hull surface reduces friction with the water and so means greater efficiency. On the other hand, standard ship-building methods have resulted in disaster for the super-tankers for they easily break up under only moderately adverse conditions. Much heavier construction methods must be employed to hold them together, as Galileo found 400 years ago.

Materials and structure are the inhibitors to large scale due to the effects of gravity. Unless new materials are synthesized that have a larger molecular base, and new approaces to building are discovered, the very large are restricted from use on the surface of our planet, but might fare better under water. All the advantages of the things of great magnitude without any of the disadvantages might be found in outer space where a reduced surface and increased volume mean less material, and where it would not be necessary to be concerned about gravity when determining structures. As with the microbes, space objects can form with far more freedom than creatures and structures subject to the force of gravity.

4 THE FORMS OF FUNCTION

The biologists say that all morphology is adaptive, meaning that through the generations, a species will alter its form to better suit its climate, terrain, movements, food intake, fighting, mating, and all the countless circumstances that constitute its environment and its living within that environment — its functioning. The artists, designers and architects have put it another way — form follows function, meaning that the form of an object should be obedient to the necessities of its function.

Both statements mean about the same thing applied to the natural and the human environments, but both lead us to believe that there may be an end result, when in fact the process itself is the end, and the object of this process, the evolving form, could be forever changing, hoping to catch up to that elusive form of perfect obedience. (21)

Is there such a thing as complete functionality? And, if so, what possible form can accomplish this task? Let's take an example: a gardener turns the soil in a small vegetable patch. As she works she thinks of her hand shovel that had been used for so long but is now wearing out. The leading edge has been worn ragged, the wooden handle is cracked. Rust, weather, long use and strain have all extracted a portion of its life. In her mind, as she works, she rebuilds the shovel from the beginning to fit her exact needs. When she thinks back she realizes that the little shovel has not really served her well at all. Her hands were always smooth with shiny calluses, the inside of her left thumb always begins to blister after two hours, the shovel's handle is too short and thick, the blade at the wrong angle, the shovel is too heavy, dirt sticks to the blade's surface, and the whole design is really rather clumsy.

As she works with the old shovel, a new one slowly develops in her mind. It has no identification to any known material and no thought for structure. A parade of details to solve individual needs marches through her thoughts and accumulates into a totally new shovel. The emerging form is hardly reminiscent of anything ever seen before. This new shovel could be operated with one hand or two, or two hands and a foot. The slim, light handle always seems to fit the hand, no matter where it is placed, for the material of the handle is soft on its exterior but firm just below. When pressure is exerted on the handle, it flexes ever-so-slightly to add spring to the movement.

Due to the unique arrangement of the handle's end, a strong grasp can always be had without angling the wrist. But, more satisfying is the shovel's ability, without any mechanical apparatus at all, to change its length to accomodate any kind of digging. At the other end of the handle is a scoop that is curved on the front side, flat on the backside, yet thin and very strong. With almost no effort, it can slice through

73

root and clay and slip out clean, and though small, it can carry an enormous load. This new shovel grows sharper and tougher with years of work. It has a form that is so appealing that, after work, the gardener would want to hang it in her living room as a decoration. However, if left on the garden wall in the rain and snow for twenty-five years, it would gain a patina that would even increase its beauty without having one iota of a deterrent to its function. As the last shovelful came out of the ground, the gardener independently realized that form can follow but never, never catch up to function.

Can utilitarian form ever reach its goal of becoming completely obedient to its function? The answer is a definitive "no," but, just as surely, it must always try. The small hand shovel with the rusted metal and cracked wood will probably be replaced by one that is changed but little, for the adaptive process is very slow. This is a shovel that is sufficient to satisfy the needs of the undemanding buyer, but a great distance from the ideal. Even if we were to pretend that structurally and mechanically through some yet undiscovered principles it was possible to design the gardener's ideal tool, and it was possible through some yet unsynthesized artificial materials to construct it, the form would still be questionable; all those who come in contact with it would have a different opinion of an ideal shovel. The user's doctor would like it to demand the use of certain muscles and ease some movements, the garden and its beneficiaries would want the most work rendered, the store owner who sold it would look for the ease of storage and little demand for shelf space, the shippers want the lightest, smallest, the manufacturer would look for profit. And the gardener's ideal would possibly change through the passing years.

There is usually an attempt to accomplish things with the least effort and with the most successful results possible. This is the common direction of all things in a general movement toward economy. Adaptive response tends to discard the less successful (least economical in energy, form, and material) in favor of the more successful. How does adaptive morphology work for a change in the marketplace? (22)

A carpenter has a selection of four hammers. The big one is for heavy timber framing, two middle-sized are for planking and sheeting, and a small one is for cabinet work. The all function sufficiently well for their intended purpose, but the carpenter's mode of work has changed. Less and less is heavy timber-

ing required, for lighter beams are quicker to assemble and cheaper, and many times the large beams are bolted together with steel straps instead of large spikes, so the great framing hammer is left in the tool chest. The carpenter is also called upon less to make the kitchen and bathroom cabinets; they are factory-made now and only require simple installation on the job, so the delicate, finely balanced finishing hammer also rests in the tool chest.

Of the carpenter's two middle-weight hammers, he prefers one over the other for it seems better balanced, the claws are angled for easier pulling, and the handle is more comfortable. When these remaining two hammers are worn out or broken, the carpenter will look for a replacement to duplicate only the one of his preference. Presuming this carpenter's situation is repeated in other circumstances, the hardware store will have repeat orders for the now popular make and type of hammer. If the process works unimpeded, the manufacturers will cut back or cease production on the other lines of hammers, and so the adaptive process filters through the system. Two hammers were eliminated because they were overspecialized and could not tolerate a shift in usage, and they are on their way to becoming extinct. The specialization was not a hindrance, but an advantage while there was a demand for their performance. The highly specialized often enjoy comfortable niches free of competition while the situation remains stable. The non-specialized must compete as did the two middle size hammers. One of the middle-size hammers was eliminated because of a less useful form, which meant more effort and energy expended by the

4-1 A and B The term "form follows function" tends to be regarded as a design approach with an end result. But by definition it is a process in progress, that will probably never reach a conclusive end. When this small microscope was designed and used in the seventeenth century it marked a certain refinement in the art, a level of form and function for that time. The base, the thumb adjustment, the barrel and eyepiece were forms designed to fulfill a certain function within the context of this microscope. Two hundred years later the microscope with a camera attachment represented just another plateau, but major achievements in the state of the art separate the two: moving and finely adjustable stage, refinement in optics, multiple lenses and with the camera attachment the possibility of recording the image on film.

Both microscopes represent a level of technical achievement long since surpassed. The jump from optical to electronic magnification was a larger technical achievement, though it took just 20 years. The function of a microscope today remains essentially the same but the forms that have served it have changed drastically. Doubtlessly the forms of our microscopes today will be quite crude compared to the forms and needs for the new level of functional demand in the future.

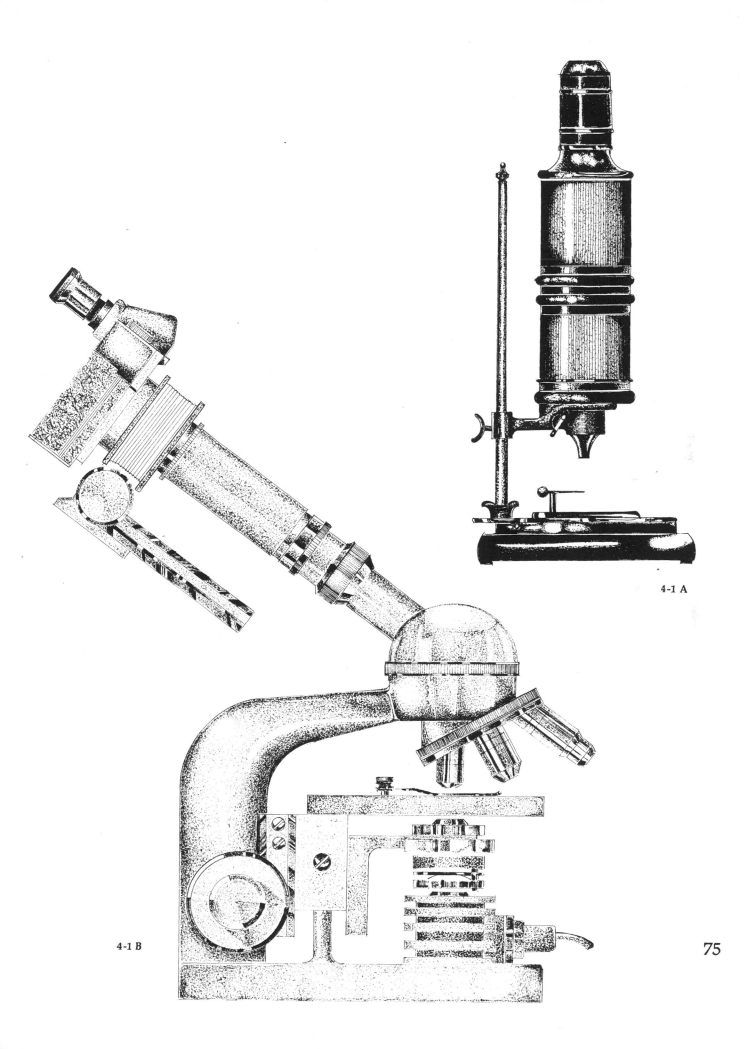

4-1 A

4-1 B

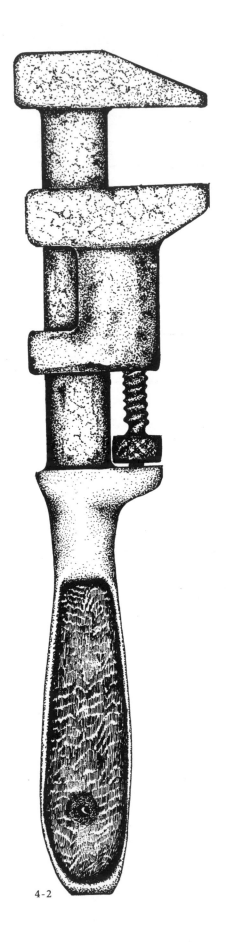

carpenter. The successful hammer must now be matched, at the market place, with new types of hammers that will appear because their creators and manufacturers believe that they have something that is superior to the existing hammers; superiority may not be in form but economics, packaging, advertising, or distribution, so the fittest tend to survive. The least suited either disappear or are changed to better compete: descent with modification.

We are inclined to accept both the natural and man-made objects that inhabit our environment as being sufficient and acceptable for their task. But the fact that this adaptive process is a functioning one means by definition that the optimal conditions have not yet been obtained. All carpenters' hammers are successful to varying degrees, but they also have many shortcomings that render them inefficient, uneconomical and, to some extent, failures.

When people who use their hands in their work become specialists and very good at their professions, they often demand tools that have a finely adjusted form. Artists have a favorite brush or palette knife; mechanics have a particular set of wrenches; masons have a special trowel; a tailor will have one best pair of shears, and the surgeon will find one instrument that seems to best fulfill the needs because of its superior form. The differences between the magnificent tool and the mediocre tool may be slight at times and sometimes may exist more in the operator's imagination than in actuality.

R. A. Salsman cites an early 19th century European example of this expressed need for refinement of tool. "Not only do tradesmen living in different districts demand different varieties of tools but, fortunately or unfortunately for the tool-makers, there are strange inconsistencies. For instance, the Coopers' axe used in the Liege District of Belgium is precisely the same shape as the English coach-builder's axe. While the ordinary cooper's axe is also used in many parts of Europe, no English wheelwright or coach-builder would dream of using a cooper's axe for trimming spokes or wedges."

4-2 For years this adjustable wrench was the only one to be found at the marketplace. With the appearance of a new type that was more versatile, angled better, and less clumsy (see illustration #4-4), repeat purchase orders dwindled on the old type; manufacturers ceased production, and it became obsolete. If it could have been improved to better compete with the new model it might have survived, but as it was the selective process of improvement left it in the past.

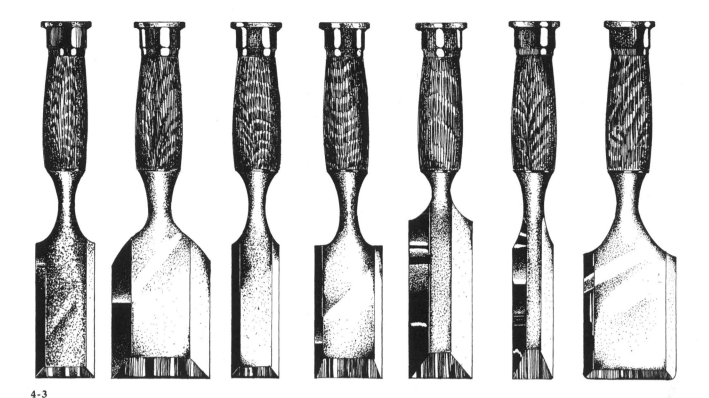

4-3

During the final half of the nineteenth century and into the twentieth century, the skilled hand trades reached a high degree of perfection. Salsman writes, "The village tradesman developed a tradition of skill and an instinctive talent for good design. A very high level of workmanship and design was maintained. Wherever one goes it is scarcely possible to find a poorly-made cart or plow, badly forged harrow, or shoddy work in saddlery or harnesses." (23)

To produce this artistry, the tradesmen became absorbed in their work and so their tools became extremely important to them. They had definite ideas about the form and function of their tools and so demanded an enormous variety of tools for every conceivable function. Quotes Salsman again, "The 1905 catalog of William Hunt and Son, among others, illustrates 42 different shapes of billhook, intended for laying hedges, culling gorse, chopping firewood, and so on. The mail order house of Belknap (American) lists over 40 varieties of felling axe, each in six or more sizes ... In 1850 a firm of York plane makers listed 29 distinct varieties of moulding planes alone, and each variety was made in five or more sizes ... 24 distinct varieties (of chisels) were listed by a well-known London tool merchant about 1900, each with its own range of style and size."

More interesting than the fact that there was such an enormous variety of size, style and make of

4-3 Skilled craftsmen of the late 19th century demanded perfection in their tools, which meant not only tools of good materials and workmanship, but an enormous selection. These seven chisels are only part of a cabinetmaker's selection of flat chisels. To these are added many varieties of rounded chisels, and then all the other ranks of tools: planes, saws, hammers, augers, and many tools that are unknown to us today.

similar tools is the question of why there was such a demand. The answer seems to be two-fold. As already mentioned, the tradesmen cared about their work and its results so each slight change was meaningful and, in turn, the tool that performed that change had to be what the tradesmen thought was the best form.

The second factor, tradition, actually became an inhibition of a function/form agreement. As the local blacksmiths gave way to the growing industrial centers, the new large companies had to absorb many local traditional tool forms from the blacksmiths they replaced. The indigenous blacksmith had followed the specific demands of the tradition-bound trades. At times the forms of similar items were considerably different over the next hill, a few miles distance.

It is peculiar that the artisans would allow a condition such as tradition to become a factor to prevent the development of the better form when there was such an expressed desire for refinement. This paradox seems to point out the sometimes arbitrary nature of the concept of the "best" form. Each trades-

77

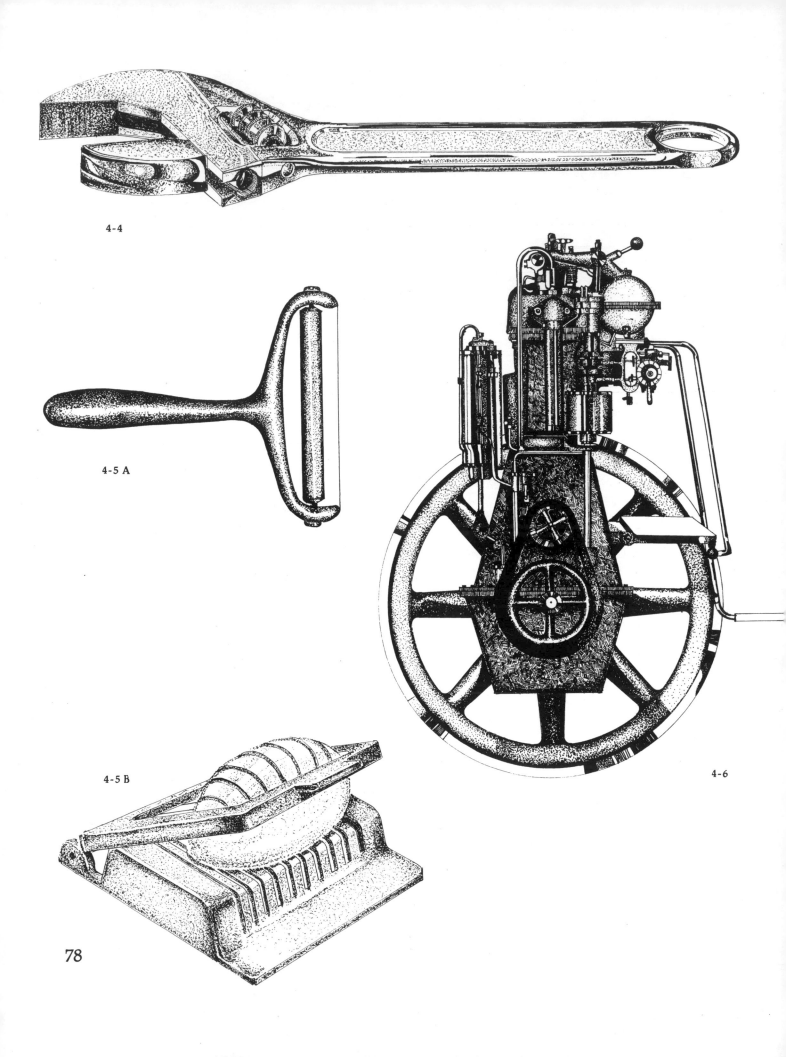

4-4

4-5 A

4-5 B

4-6

78

man probably thought, rather complacently, that he must be using the superior tool, and the toolmaker, perhaps somewhat begrudgingly, honored the wants of each.

The above might serve as an example of many forms for a given function. We see the opposite of this developing today — one form for many functions. The multi-purpose tool is a popular notion in the general market now for its economy, space-saving, and portability. These multi-purpose tools are generally used by the non-professional worker, whose involvement is temporary. Furniture, carpentry and mechanics tools, kitchen supplies, gardening and camping equipment, office and business equipment all come in makes and models that are advertised to perform many tasks. If the task is relatively easy and not specialized, one tool can replace a large number of tools and perform the job sufficiently well. The adjustable wrench works well enough for the non-specialized job. With only a slight change of its form, it can replace a large set of fixed wrenches. (24)

It could be generalized that the simpler the form is, the larger the number of non-specific functions it can perform. In the kitchen drawer can usually be found a hand cheese cutter, a frame which becomes the handle and holds a roller and the wire cutter. This item, compared to a teaspoon, is rather complex. The cheese cutter is made to cut cheese. This it does rather well, but it really can only be used for this one function. The simpler form of the spoon is suitable for many uses: beating and stirring, eating, measuring, dealing with dry and liquid materials, and reaching into things to scoop. A large flat table knife, a yet

4-4 At one time during the height of the artisan economy, hand tools were very specialized. The tendency is in the other direction now, for more multi-purpose tools, one tool that will fulfill many functions. The adjustable wrench is an example of one single tool that is capable of replacing a whole set of wrenches. The anticipated trade-off is a lack of proficiency. Usually the non-specialized object does not perform as well.

4-5 A and B The cheese cutter, and even more so the egg slicer, are highly specialized objects, excellently adapted to a single task but almost unusable for anything else. The very specialized tool is usually of a complex form.

4-6 This old diesel engine operated in a pumping station outside London for almost eighty years of continuous sevice. As admirably as it did function, it was only capable of one task: providing rotary motion. It was suited for nothing else. Its form is highly complex and its function is very specialized.

4-7 A, B, C The spoon, an uncomplex form, is usable for many more tasks than the ones for which it was designed. The hollow hemisphere is yet a simpler form and capable of performing an even greater range of functions. The plank and two sawhorses, regarded as an alterable tool, can be changed to become more specific in its form and function.

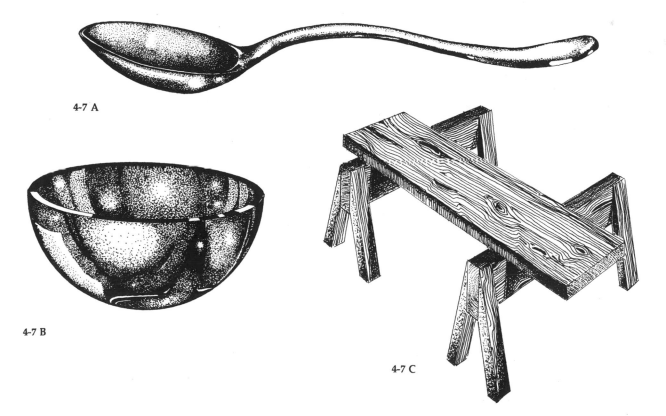

4-7 A

4-7 B

4-7 C

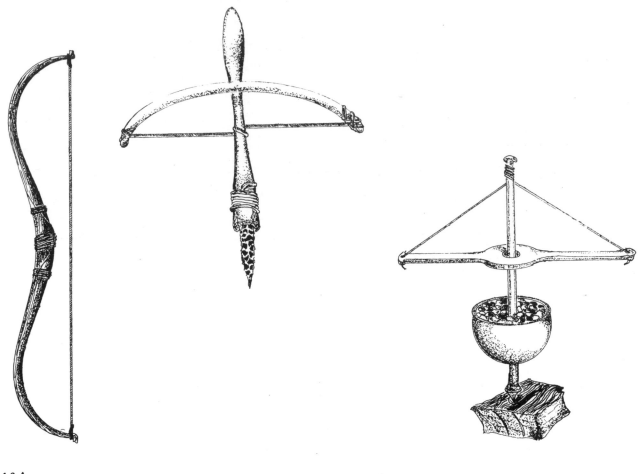

4-8 A

simpler form, can perform all those tasks plus chopping, sawing, dicing, spreading, prying cans, screw driving, and slicing materials, including cheese. Most of these tasks will not be accomplished as well as a more specialized tool can perform them, but this is the anticipated trade-off.

David Pye, the design theorist, has worked with this notion. He asks, "What is the activity proper to a straight cylindrical bar of steel a quarter inch in diameter on cross-section and four inches long? What function is this form following, or ought it follow? Of course, you could use it for an enormous number of different purposes but then, for nearly every one of them, you could use something different equally well." (25)

The four inch steel bar represents a single form which has the potential for many functions. The reverse might also be found: a single function produced by many different forms and having different purposes. Take the example of the function of transferring motion through a flexible belt to a shaft. The linear movement of the belt causes the shaft to rotate.

As early as Paleolithic times, rotary motion was effected by the bow drill, a sinew or thong stretched between the ends of a bent bow, and twisted about a verticle spindle. As the bow is run back and forth, the spindle rotates. The early forms of this were used to drill holes, and the spinning friction used to kindle fires. One of the next steps in the bow drill's evolutionary process was a lathe. The bow this time rotated the work between two horizontal points in the lathe.

In these two forms, the rotary motion was partial or discontinuous. The object spun as the bow moved in one direction, then stopped and reversed its rotation as the bow moved back again. Next the bow disappeared and the sinew was replaced by a continuous cord or belt powered by hand, animal, wind or water, and the rotation became constant. In this form, the mechanism has a two-fold use: the transfer of rotary movement from one place to another, and the reduction and increase of speed or power. The process is with us today, and has become a common instrument of industry. (26)

4-8 B

4-8 A and B   A form and a function can undergo drastic change while the process that makes the function possible can remain essentially the same. Shown here in five steps is the evolution of a process through many forms and functions. The process: rotary motion caused by a moving flexible belt. The hunter's bow was the probable ancestor of the bow drill. It was discovered that a slack bow string could be twisted about a spindle and moved back and forth to produce a spinning action. The rotating spindle had been used previously between the palms of the hand. The bow drill was used to bore holes and kindle fires, and it is still in use in some parts of the world. This process was then transferred to a slightly more sophisticated version, shown in the third illustration. The pump drill was held between two hands, and the horizontal bar was pulled down to unwrap the cord and spin the shaft. Momentum then wound the cord in the opposite direction and the action was repeated. The hemisphere, usually a gourd, was filled with pebbles as a flywheel. The process was then changed slightly, but with profound effect. These first examples show discontinuous rotary motion, a spinning in one direction, stopping, and a spinning in the other direction. When the flexible belt was connected to itself in a loop, the rotation became continous in one direction. The main purpose of continuous rotary motion is to transfer motion from one place to another and increase or decrease speed and power. This process has become an important part of modern technology.

There are many plants and animals that have remained unchanged through vast stretches of time while the environment about them has been in con-

stant renewal and modification. These few enduring species were highly successful from the beginning and so little refinement was required to keep them functioning and competitive. There are some highly successful man-made designs which endure remarkably well in our society. All successful forms have economy as a common factor. All forms, natural and human, that express economy seem to be the enduring ones. An economical form is one that gets the most from the least effort and energy expended, least material used, and offers the maximum return of work. Economy then becomes a key factor. But in accepting this premise, we must leave the notion that economy is only used where it must be used. It is a misconception to think that economic design is used only when something is lacking and nothing better can be afforded. Economy means efficiency. An efficient design is geared as precisely as possible to its use. All the elements work as efficiently as can be expected.

The bowline knot is one such design. When one rope is joined to another or a loop is tied at the end of

81

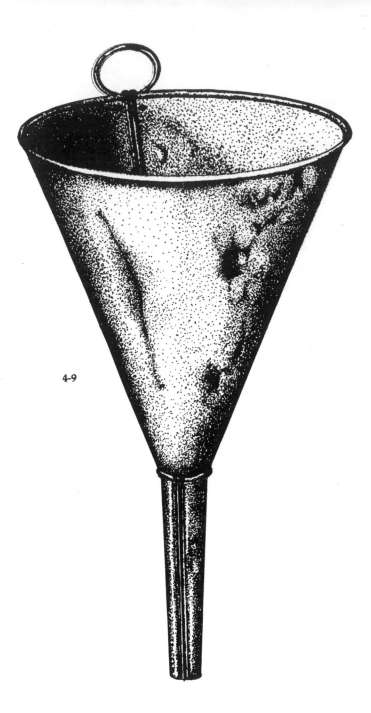

4-9

a line, experienced sailors use the bowline knot which will offer them the security of knowing that it won't slip, and yet, when wanted, will come untied with ease, no matter how much it has been tightened. Another such long lasting form is the sewing needle. It is perhaps the oldest unchanged tool still in use.

The first improvement to the sewing needle in many thousands of years came about within our time: the addition of a diagonal slit in the side of the eye to allow the thread to be snapped into place. This eliminates the difficulties of pushing the end of thread through the hole. The bicycle has evolved to a high level of form-function-need alignment. In comparison to other means of transportation, a human upon the bicycle ranks extraordinarily high in efficiency. The sailboat has gone through a long process of evolution, from awkward craft that could only sail before the wind, to the racing yachts of today, actually able to sail faster than the wind on some tacks.

4-9 A few very long-lasting and very beautiful forms have been with us unchanged since their inception. These elegant forms have endured because they answer the needs in the simplest, most direct way, and usually they are very economical of material. Whether sheet metal, plastic, or glass, the shape of the funnel reinforces the strength of the material because of its conical form. Additionally, it is suited to the sheet metal layout and rolling processes of fabrication. The form of the funnel tends to spiral the liquid from the larger opening to the smaller opening, thus speeding its passage. Finally, the design is visually articulate, the very form of the funnel speaks of its purpose.

4-10 The bowline knot is another example of an elegant design. It is almost impossible to cause it to slip. But many knots can boast of this ability. Most other knots, though, become so tightly intwined after a hard pull that they are very difficult to break loose. The bowline knot can almost always come apart with ease, and its simplicity makes it easy to tie. The knot has a quality that other designs might envy: it becomes stronger as greater force is placed on it, rather than weaker.

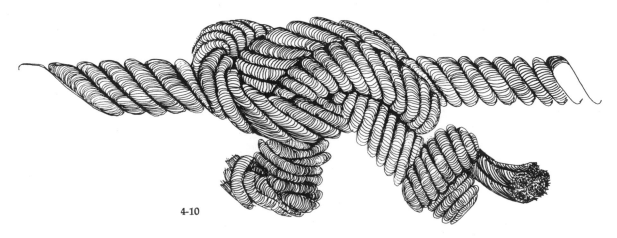

4-10

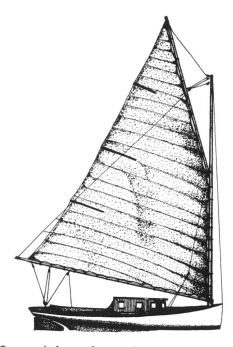

Some of these elegant forms can be found in our society; some are from other societies and times. Some remain in the same culture in which they originated; others have passed from culture to culture. Most are simple of form like rock climbing tools and Eskimo bone implements; others are strong and light like umbrellas and kayaks; still others are very efficient like sailboats, wheelbarrows and gliders. But all are honest designs that are direct, have a clarity of function, and deliver the very most from the very least. (27)

There are many ways of regarding function: what it does, how it operates, how it changes and how time

4-11 A and B Another way of considering form and function is in terms of input and output. The function changes the state of things and the form controls that change. A pair of scissors transforms something that is in a continuous state, a sheet of paper, or a piece of fabric, into two or more separate things, the scissors bringing about the separation. The reverse is true of the measuring cup — it brings together. The measuring cup transforms an uncontained volume of liquid into a measured and contained quantity.

4-11 B

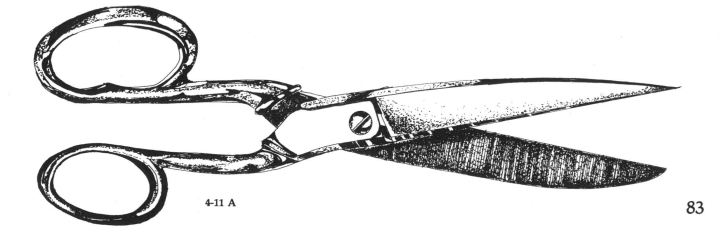

4-11 A

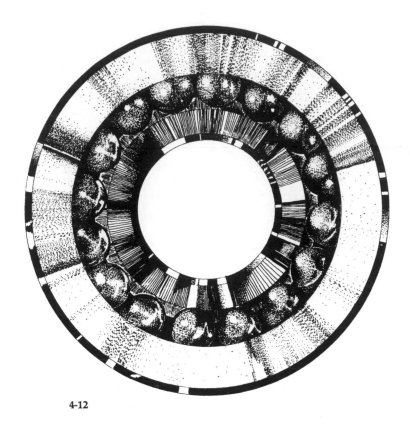

4-12

and change in turn affect function. At its simplest level, function can be regarded as merely change; that which goes into that which functions will, by definition, have to be different from that which comes out. The function of a wood stove is to produce heat. The input is wood, fire and oxygen; the output is heat, ash and carbon dioxide. The input to a crab claw is potential food; the output is ordered food delivered to the mouth of a creature.

Cross- and trans-functionalism are yet two more considerations. A well-antlered elk is a model of functional design when fighting an adversary. The spreading powerful antlers can overwhelm another with a lesser growth, or throw a hungry wolf aside. But the wide heavy girth of the antlers proves to be a disastrous burden when speed is needed in a dense forest. This is cross-functionalism. The elk suffers from cross-functional action, for the antlers serve him adequately in one situation, when confronted by his adversaries, but restrict him in another situation, by catching snags while he runs through a thick forest.

Cross-functionalism works for one cause, but against another. The tallest tree in a forest is the one that will benefit from the most rain, spread its wind-borne seeds the farthest, but it could be struck by lightning and the first to go down in an ice storm or gale. Trans-functionalism has almost the opposite

result. It unites two or more systems of action that might otherwise conflict when and where they come together. A traffic light very graphically performs a trans-functional service by smoothly coordinating conflicting lanes of moving cars where they cross one another. Membranes, barrier reefs, mangrove colonies and other such interface systems, perform trans-functional services by blending together two opposing forces.

We cannot accept the concept of function as change without considering time, for change and time are almost synonymous. How can we look at an object and question its function without accounting for the context of that function in time and change. In the volumetric series *Towards a Theoretical Biology*, David Bohm has placed the order of things in three categories: the Quasi-equilibrium, the Dynamic, and the Creative Process. He continues by saying, "As a rule, we tend to begin in a situation close to equilibrium, which enables us to recognize certain relatively static or constant features of Process. We give these features names." At this point we can imagine a full ripe fruit as it is picked from the tree, placed on a table and called an apple. "...and are

84

thus led to regard them as stable objects or entities. Then, as we see that these features are changing and transforming ..." Thus we imagine that the apple is not eaten but removed to the shelf where it shrivels, and, if neglected, eventually deteriorates into an almost unrecognizable lump of mildew and darkened substance. Bohm continues, "we seek to explain their relative stability in terms of a dynamic process of interaction of some basic entities." In our example, since we neglected to eat the apple ourselves, we soon realize that its molecules will succumb to other processes of consumption. Bohm concludes, "Still later we come to the notion of a creative process, in which there are no basic objects, entities, or substances, but in which all that is to be observed comes into existence as a certain order, remains relatively stable for some time, and then passes out of existence." (28)

The apple was only a fleeting form that very briefly reached the level at which it received the question, "What is the function of an apple?" before it passed into a totally new form and finally a new substance.

To state that change is the only permanent feature of our existence is, in itself, a gross oversimplification; the order of change is altering continually and, in turn, these new points of departure produce totally new features of change. Change, in other words, is itself changing; possibly the total process is too vast for us to comprehend. To the insect that lives for sixteen hours, the life of a morning glory is vast. To man, the life or stability of a sequoia tree is vast; but in geologic terms, the mountains, planets or solar systems are fleeting. As is the apple, we too are moving swiftly through time and change, and the apple's passing shadow can be comprehended as a relatively stable entity to us.

4-13 Function and form cannot be considered without regard to time, for time affects form, which affects its function. The shriveled tangerine certainly will have a different function now compared to when it was plucked from the tree.

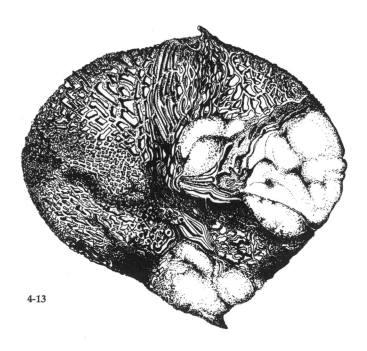

4-13

5 THE GENERATIONS
Influences from the Past

When the pre-toolmaking humans came out of the forest into the open, their bodies and brains responded. In the open, only their legs were responsible for mobility. Their feet became adapted for walking and their hands dangled idly at their sides, free to hold and carry, pick up objects and manipulate them. But life was dangerous in the open and the idly held stone found a purpose. Since neither speed of flight nor strength of attack was a quality of the humans, the stone became their weapon for defense and offense. Rocks, branches, and bones were first used as they were found; then they were improved by accident, and finally by intent. (29)

There is a measured sequence of discovery, invention, and influence as chance, time and purposeful observation effect change. Though it may take a tremendous length of time, discovery by chance is simply effected by simple brains, but the recognition of the value of the discovery requires intelligence. It is intelligence that gives the ability to evaluate results, discard the useless, and retain the useful; the accident is intentionally repeated. This then becomes the very first step in tool using.

There is an enormous difference between the sharp edged rock that was found and used as a cutting tool, and the round rock intentionally broken to produce a sharp edge. Probably at first, the found tools were purposely sorted and the best shapes were selected, then by accident it was found that these more desirable forms could be obtained when one stone was broken against another. The procedure was then accomplished with intent, and this sequence has been called *Primary Mutation*. After the discovery has been established, change usually occurs through accident or intent to improve the function. This is called *Free Mutation*. An early farmer improved the digging stick by the use of a branch stub. Improperly trimmed, it was discovered to serve as a foot holder

5-1 Monumental significance — would be a conservative judgement to place upon the importance of the very first generation of human artifacts, the first crafted tools. There is a vast difference between the sharp pointed rock that was found and used, and the rock willfully flaked and turned into a tool by purposely directed acts. The former only requires observation and selective vision; the latter requires the selective rationale plus a knowledge of the nature of the material that is being worked, and more important a hand, brain, eye dexterity and coordination.

5-2 The sequence of tool use was probably the following: discovery of an object, a bone, branch or stone, which was used as a tool without alteration to its form; the stone or branch was then purposefully turned into a tool by shaping it to the desired form; and finally, an improvement was made to the tool. This last step is significant because often the improvement grew out of the use of the tool, rather than something suggested by an existing form, as the flaked tool was suggested by the found tool. The hafting of implements is such a case. The stone tools were uncomfortable on the hand due to sharp edges, and so were wrapped with skins, the skins actually forming the first handles. Short sections of wood probably replaced the skins because the wood was more durable. It may then have been found by accident that if a longer wooden handle were attached to the stone it could be wielded with greater power and speed. So the hafted axe was born.

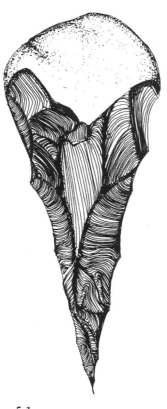

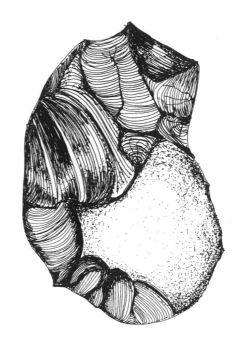

5-1

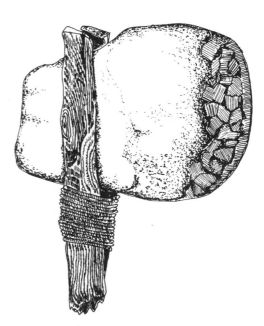

5-2

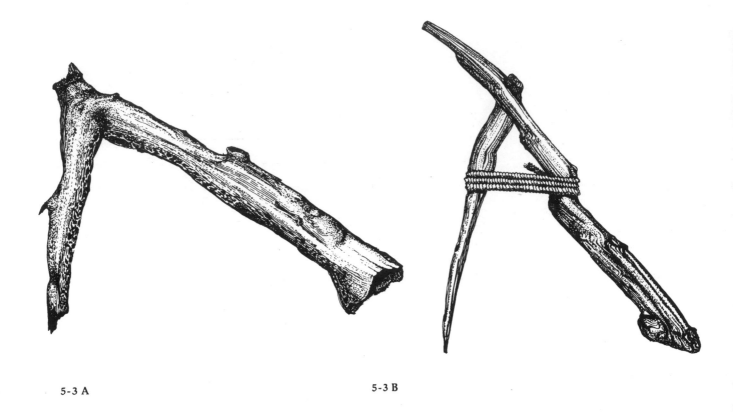

5-3 A   5-3 B

allowing the foot to assist the arms in pushing the stick into the ground.

Substitution is another method of change. It defines the switching of materials while the concept remains the same — the substitution of the stone pointed spear for the wooden one, or the evolution of the sewing needle, from bone to brass and bronze to iron and steel. (30)

In early times Primary Mutation and Free Mutation accounted for the majority of development and improvement, but as the quantity of knowledge grew larger, and new basic discoveries became less frequent, *Cross Mutation* became the dominant force of change, as it is today. Cross Mutation is a re-adaptation of an idea or device from one artifact to another; the potter's wheel to the spinning wheel, or the bowdrill to the firemaker.

But the path of invention and discovery has been amazingly slow. The simplest of devices seem to have eluded the imagination of whole societies for centuries. Immediacy of solution may have been one of the reasons for this. Invention is most easily effected on a very direct basis: a need arises, a discovery is made, the invention follows and it is employed directly. The use of most early tools and weapons came about this way. The inventions responded to dilemmas and cir-

5-3 A and B In the process of tool development 200 millions years may have passed between the arising of a need and the tool to fill that need. But then, improvement to the tool may have come relatively quickly, for the form of the improvement could have been suggested by the existing tool that was replaced. Such is the case with this hoeing implement. It was taken from a tree section in its original form. The improved tool was made from two sections of wood joined to form a similar but lighter and more easily handled hoe.

5-4 In the evolutionary process there are many methods of invention and discovery that cut the wasteful and repetitious process of building knowledge and losing it again (see text). One of them is called substitution; this refers to the transferring of a form and concept through a series of materials. The curving bone served as an early draw knife; the inside was sharpened as a cutting edge. Used in the same way, the knife then was translated over the centuries into bronze, wrought iron and steel.

cumstances of the moment. It takes more insight and planning to invent when there is no apparent application at hand. The round tree trunk served as a roller thousands of years before the wheel and axle came into existence. The tree trunk was direct, but the wheel requires cutting, centering, boring, the making of an axle, mounting the axle, and generally extensive planning. The solution is not immediate.

It is very likely that the wheel, as with all primary inventions, was found many, many times over in early societies only to have the observation unrecognized as one of significance; it may even have been

88

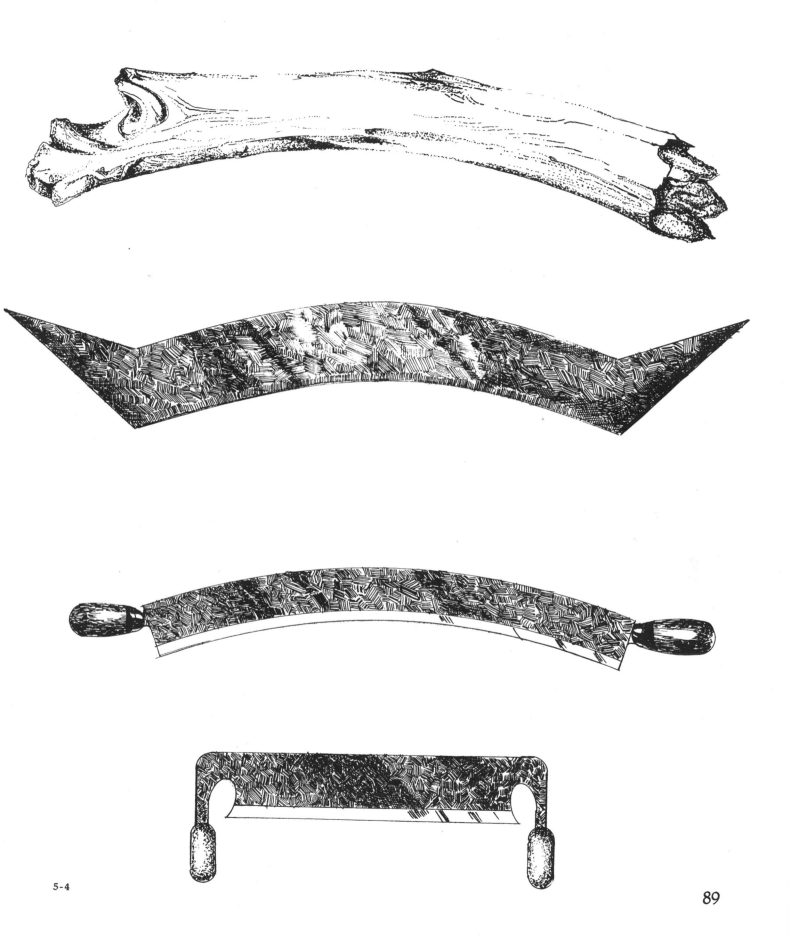

ing that they might possess dramatic possibilities, but finding it impossible to put them to use. These must wait for another decade or century for their matrix of employment.

Human technology often develops in surprisingly and unaccountably different basic ways. In the western societies, most cutting action by hand tool is in a movement away from the body; saws cut as the arm straightens out, moving the saw away; planes, chisels, knives, and gouges are all directed to cut as they are pushed from the shoulders and chest. The eastern societies have taken an opposite turn. Their tools are set to cut as they are drawn to the body. Why these important differences began can only be ascribed to chance.

The reverse of this situation is also common. It has occurred in the distant past that similar creative

used in isolated events only to be lost again for centuries. Then as now it takes the keenest of minds to visualize the potential and possible applications of an abstract invention. History must be filled with incidents of important pivotal discoveries that were unapplied and unfulfilled, and again dropped into oblivion. Individuals, companies, and scientists today may be handling curious theories and ideas, feel-

5-5 Cross-mutation is a blending of ideas and technologies, or a readaption of discoveries. The motion of a wheel spinning on an axle blended with the use of sails on a boat to receive the thrust of the wind became the sail powered windmill found in Mediterranean countries.

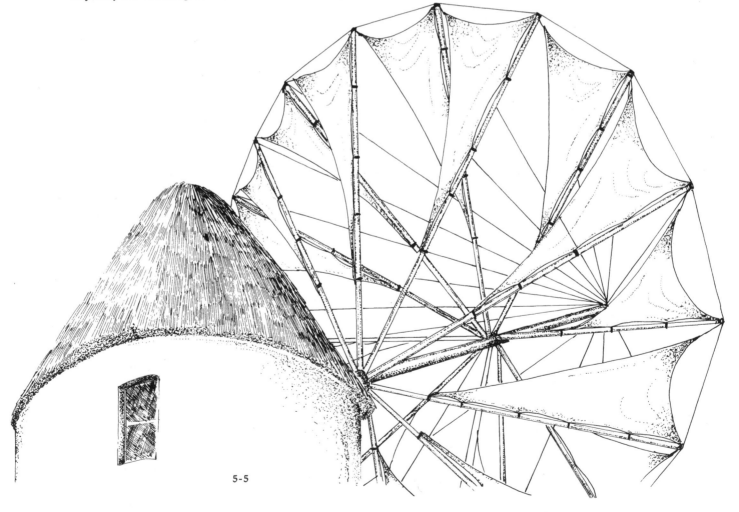

5-5

5-6 A

5-6 B

5-6 The American buck saw, as with all saws and most tools of the western societies, operates with the cutting stroke being the one that is pushed away from the body. The Japanese *ryoba* saw cuts, as all Japanese saws, as it is pulled into the body. There are advantages and disadvantages to both methods. Of interest, though, is the totally diverse actions that arose in the East and West. There seems to be little to account for these differences or their persistence other than chance of discovery and the tyranny of tradition carrying on.

discoveries spontaneously and simultaneously emerge from parts of the world removed and out of contact from one another. Why this happens is speculation but it is easy to look at the possible causes. Observation of technologies in the natural world must have accounted for a great deal of influence. People observed nest building, digging, a floating insect, the bending arm, the joint of a crab claw. These are a few of the thousands of observations that were doubtlessly effective in opening insights. Would humans have developed aircraft without flying insects and birds, milkweed seeds, or maple samara as models, or submarines without fish and porpoise, tension bridges without spiderwebs? Probably so, but it likely would have taken much

more time. Without doubt wheeled vehicles would have come about far earlier in civilization had the wheel existed in nature.

The human body itself must have been a strong determination on tool use, size and form. The actions of hammering, grasping, cutting, and scraping, holding, squashing and splitting, bending and joining, piercing and boring, sharpening, measuring, and making have been called by many different grunts that evolved into names and words from continent to continent for thousands of centuries of technonogy. Through these actions humankind has altered the materials of its environment. These actions entail certain kinds of movements: swinging, twisting, pushing and pulling, and squeezing.

The hand is capable of a discontinuous rotary motion. The lower portion of the forearm consists of two bones, the ulna and the radius. These bones are able to twist in their sockets slightly crossing which enables a 180 degree rotation of the hand. With a back and forth twisting motion, simple boring can be accomplished with a hand held tool. This action probably accounted for the first rotary tools.

91

The arms, the legs, the shoulders, and the back move best in certain patterns. Most craft work is done by the hands and the arms. The hands hold and direct the tool and work the materials, and the arms with the shoulders provide the power. Tool dimension and form have been regulated by size and shape of the human hand, length and strength of the arm, power of the leg, focus of the eye, and directioning of vision. With these actions so clearly defined, it would seem a fair guess that tools would evolve with similar forms when used in conjunction with these actions.

The possibilities of corresponding artifacts developing in distant corners of the world increases when there is a like climate and vegetation; geology and geography which provide similar materials for tool making and human needs. The coincidence of timing can only be ascribed to the development of parallel technologies having like needs that arise at the same time.

The fumblings of early minds and coarse hands brought the first artifacts into existence. The primary generations of tools were the products of accident, need, and the occasion of the moment. After the form and method were established all those to follow were created under the influence of this inherent technology. Patterns of decoration, shelter forms, plowshares, eating utensils, calligraphy, and all the thousands of things in early societies evolved with a resemblance to the artifacts that preceded them. The precedent broke the barrier of primary mutation, but left its legacy.

True creation, causing something to exist that has not before, is rare indeed, and some would say impossible. Most creation is a product of insight. Creation is the ability to see the ordinary within a new context; or the ability to combine known agencies to cause something new, or apparently new, to come into existence. Both these methods have roots in the past. The past has made the invention possible, but it has also influenced its outcome.

Circumstances, needs, materials, environment, observation, intelligence, and time cause primary mutation; but after the first act is created, that which follows it must forever be indebted, as influence modified by change and improvement cascades down through the centuries.

At first, societies in isolation built upon their own knowledge, and information was passed in a linear fashion from generation to generation. As societies gradually moved over the continents and between the land masses, technologies that had been developed indigenously were blended with other technologies. This process is called *Diffusion*. Usually the results of this double influencing are profoundly better than their predecessors. With diffusion, knowledge was no longer accumulated from one direction only; but as a branching stream, it poured from multiple sources into one channel of resolution.

Diffusion has increased as fast as migration, transportation, and communication allows it. Diffusion has effectively turned individual pockets of

5-7 There is often speculation about the origin of technical knowledge, whether it is by multiple invention occurring in many parts of the world simultaneously or whether it is spread by diffusion, the information traveling with migrating peoples. The blowgun is one such item in question. It is found throughout Southeast Asia, in Indonesia, and the Malay Peninsula, and also in South America. The long hunting blowgun must be rather complex, for its construction requires the joining of two or more pieces of reed, giant grass, or bamboo. Similar methods of construction are used in all these locations.

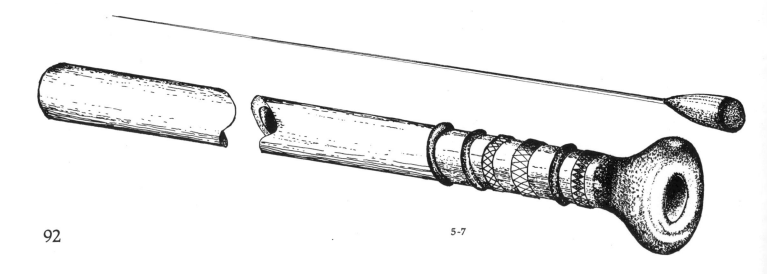

5-7

knowledge into a world knowledge. Today there is a trans-social technology that becomes more pervasive each year. We have reached our level of sophistication on the shoulders of diffusion; but is diffusion something that can be "used up?" Like entropy, can it lead us to an eventual morass of sameness without the spark of deviance? Has the diffusion of technology actually run out? (31)

In the biological context, when new growth is drawn from a limited genetic pool by mating closely related individuals, the results often show defects which are compounded because they are possessed by both parents. Biologists call this inbreeding. Mating of individuals of distant relation is called outcrossing. When breeders intentionally select individuals of distant relationship for various desirable attributes and breed them together, usually superior stock is achieved; this is called hybrid vigor. The products from the diffusion of early societies exhibited hybrid vigor—something greater than the sum of both technologies. If we had the opportunity today to diffuse with another civilization of equal technical stature from another world, the results would probably be very healthy to both.

Can we judge the value of this legacy from the past? Ideas are the heart of a civilization. As the accumulation of knowledge becomes greater, the possibility of profoundly significant contribution becomes less; less because in a matured branch of technology most of the primary discoveries and inventions have been found, while the new technologies seethe with discovery and profit from diffusion. The old, through cross mutation, must borrow ideas from close relatives (inbreeding). Most scientific creators today work in teams of highly trained professionals, and have at their disposal banks of memory with fingertip knowledge. Their work has excluded the layman, not through intent but through its own complexity. Vast quantities of knowledge must be processed in order to accumulate and sift out the pertinent facts to effect even the slightest advance.

Even at this level of current technology, individual names still come forward with impressive achievements as solitary thinkers. Generally these people concentrate on areas that are outside the sphere of modern science, areas with little prior inquiry, left out because of discredit or neglect. But the promise of primary discovery still exists, and possibly more for the individual than the team scientists, for the scientific community has gained a level of credibility that excludes questionable research. The lone scientists can gamble on taking a remote path, one which would lead not to another technical achievement, but to a totally new pasture of inquiry.

When our technology was still adolescent, Thomas Edison passed through a period during the height of his productivity in which he averaged a scientific invention a day, a total of 1,093 patents during his lifetime; many of these inventions became the first product of a whole industry to follow.

Edison had little formal education, but he did not need to accumulate facts from the past, for he and his small cluster of colleagues were at the crest of their technology. The only prerequisites they needed were the basic physical laws, knowledge of which they gained en route. "Everything is so new," wrote Edison, "that each step is in the dark. I have to make dynamos, the lamps, the conductors, and attend to a thousand details the world never hears of." Edison was referring to the system he put together that surrounded his invention of a commercially viable electric light, the only part the public was really conscious of, in the complete industry developed to create and conduct electricity into the homes.

Isaac Newton, 200 years before Edison, opened not industries but defined laws. Galileo before him investigated whole new sciences. And Archimedes, centuries before, was one of the first individuals to state that there was such a thing as science and technology. These men are found within their own time spans, each in chronological sequence with a more specialized but narrower scope. "Some say that since Archimedes of Syracuse, the causes and laws of all things have been known ... he above all handled every subject with extraordinary penetration." Archimedes founded both the disciplines of geometry and mathematics, and with a theoretical approach determined many basic mechanical principles.

Though these men of early science were highly creative individuals, often working in unsympathetic and even hostile environments, they were not supermen, and were possibly no greater than their counterparts today. They were able to effect such profound results because their answers were at hand, like the first and most easily uncovered Easter eggs at the hunt.

The restless human spirit wants change, and the changes does not always result in improvement. Often the artifacts that are the objects of this change

93

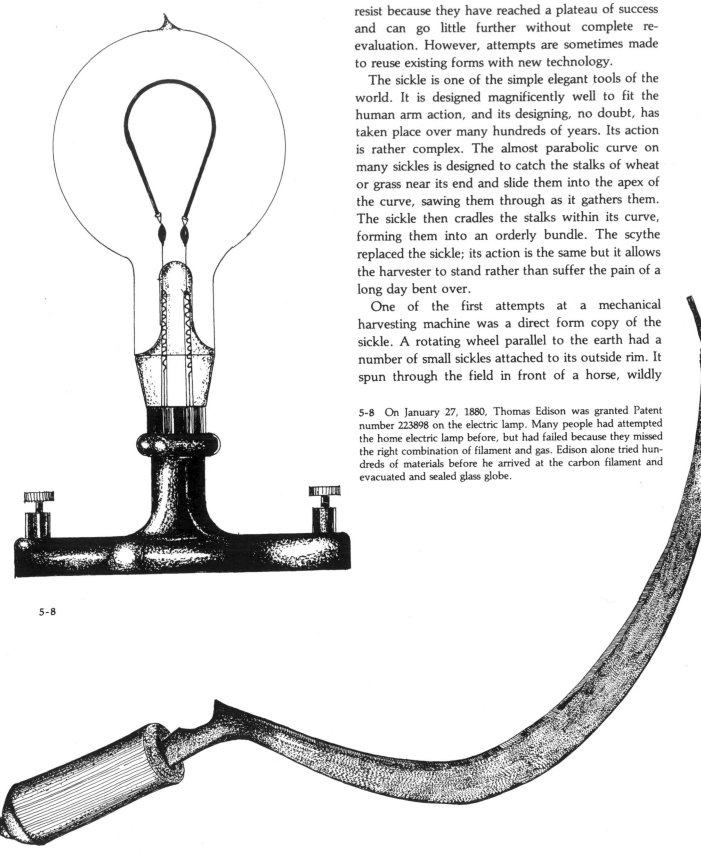

resist because they have reached a plateau of success and can go little further without complete re-evaluation. However, attempts are sometimes made to reuse existing forms with new technology.

The sickle is one of the simple elegant tools of the world. It is designed magnificently well to fit the human arm action, and its designing, no doubt, has taken place over many hundreds of years. Its action is rather complex. The almost parabolic curve on many sickles is designed to catch the stalks of wheat or grass near its end and slide them into the apex of the curve, sawing them through as it gathers them. The sickle then cradles the stalks within its curve, forming them into an orderly bundle. The scythe replaced the sickle; its action is the same but it allows the harvester to stand rather than suffer the pain of a long day bent over.

One of the first attempts at a mechanical harvesting machine was a direct form copy of the sickle. A rotating wheel parallel to the earth had a number of small sickles attached to its outside rim. It spun through the field in front of a horse, wildly

5-8 On January 27, 1880, Thomas Edison was granted Patent number 223898 on the electric lamp. Many people had attempted the home electric lamp before, but had failed because they missed the right combination of filament and gas. Edison alone tried hundreds of materials before he arrived at the carbon filament and evacuated and sealed glass globe.

5-8

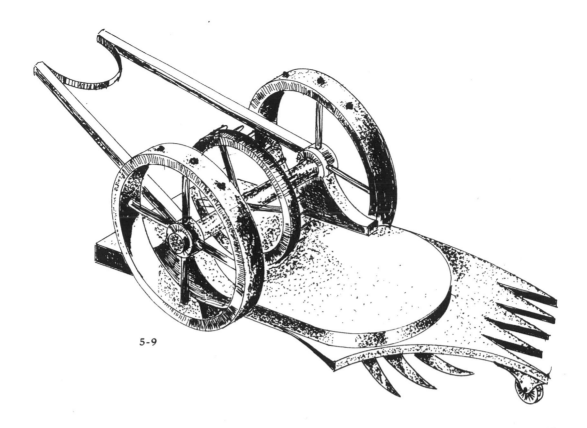

5-9

whirling the harvest to the ground. The results must have been chaotic, for instead of the sophisticated single-stroke gathering and bundling action of the sickle, it continuously cut and left behind a tangle of refuse. This machine was replaced by a device that used miniature sickles on an endless chain and with little improvement. The departure came with a change in principle that was designed after the motion of the machine rather than a re-adaptation of the hand action. A scissor-like cutter was developed by McCormick and others, and so mechanical harvesting began a totally new lineage suited to machine action. The great modern combines used in wheat farming today employ the same action as did the old McCormick reaper.

The first flight of man was attempted through the use of flapping bird wings harnessed to human arms. One of the first steam engines was powered by a boiler in the form of a human body. The movement of the engine came from steam issuing from the mouth and rotating a turbine.

The inventors of many horseless machine powered vehicles felt it necessary to enclose their power source in a covered frame resembling a draft animal. When the washing of clothes shifted from a hand operation to a machine process, several varieties of washing

5-9 This device was designed to be pushed before the horse as a mower. It employed sickle-like cutters that rapidly rotated above the ground. The inventor of this mower directly copied the human arm action rather than reinterpreting the cutting action in a form that would better suit the machine.

machines were designed after the hand operation with a pair of mechanical hands that wrung and squeezed the wash in a direct anatomical translation.

These are examples of innovations attempting to arise from under the strong influence of their predecessors. Clarity of function is forsaken because set methods and forms have clouded intelligent response; hence the appropriate use of the machine is not discovered.

Yet another example of the negative aspects of inherent technology is the design that suffers because it does not change to accommodate a change in use. The following is an example.

Clam diggers in the New England States and the Maritime Provinces have evolved a small skiff to move them onto the smooth tidewater mudflats for their clams. The skiff has slightly flaring sides and a flat bottom that curves up to the bow and stern. It has no keel at all. This small boat can carry one man and his day's digging of clams in two inches of water over a flooding clam flat; or, if left behind by the

95

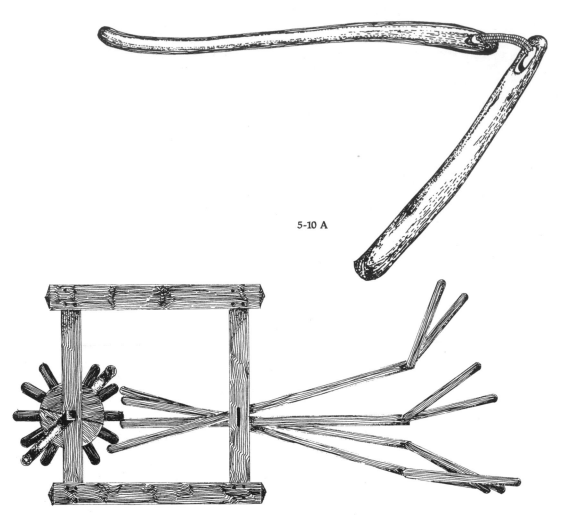

5-10 A

5-10 B

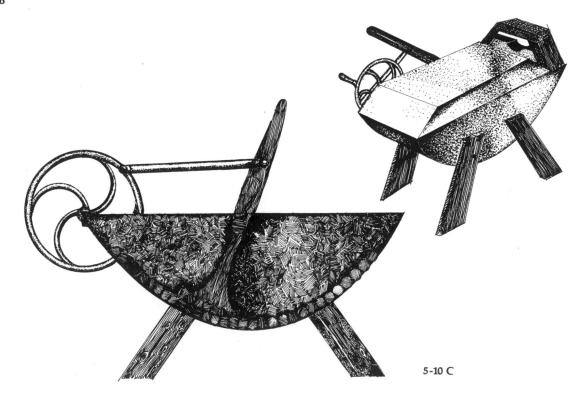

5-10 C

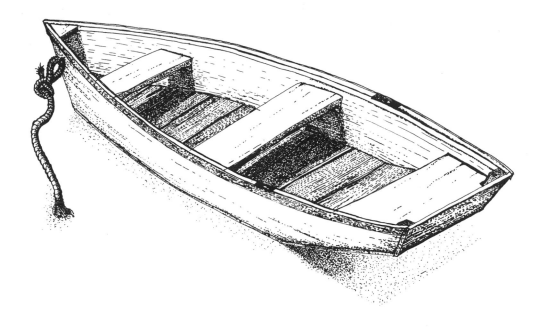

receding tide, the skiff can be pulled as a sled behind a walker with no effort at all—for the bowed, keelless flat bottom skims over the mud without causing a suction.

The boat is made from two wide pine planks for sides, joined at the bow and curved around the center seat to a narrower stern. The flare of the sides is the natural formation of the bending boards. A good skiff builder can put one together in five hours. The skiff was perfectly designed to be propelled by hand-powered oar, and, with its use of materials, the clamming skiff is completely successful. Hence there is lit-

5-10 A, B, C Usually the first generation of new devices relies heavily upon its predecessors. In the translation from hand to machine many awkward inventions attempted to translate a human or animal motion directly to a mechanism.

Separating the grain from the stalk, threshing, has been one of the basics of agriculture as long as tilling the soil has existed. The flail is an ancient tool used for this purpose. It consists of two poles tied loosely together. One is the handle; the other is beaten against the harvested crop to knock off the grain. One of the first mechanical threshers mounted several long-handled flails on a rack with a drum and pins. The drum rotated, causing the flails to rise and drop. This inefficient method was forgotten when a threshing device was discovered that was better suited to machine action. One of the early washing machines duplicated the action of the hands on a scrub board. The moving agitator, which came much later, was a more sophisticated solution.

tle reason not to follow the lineage as long as the demands remain unchanging.

However, after the proliferation of the detachable marine engine, the clam diggers have used outboard motors to run the skiffs to the flats instead of getting there by oar. Because of the swept-up and shallow stern, the motor throws the boat off balance and causes it to become awkward, dangerous, and inefficient. A faster, safer boat requires a square stern. The skiff with an outboard behind cannot be rowed with ease and cannot be pulled over the mud. The dictates of inheritance become tyrannical when custom decrees that the design thoughtlessly follow its predecessor after usage has changed and rendered it unsuccessful.

Technological development is never a steady process. Notions change and develop in fits and starts, or disappear completely. Some spring into existence suddenly with little precedent. Others accumulate over long years like limestone gathering at the tip of a stalagmite. Often development moves to a point and stops completely, for the design has reached what Siegfried Giedion has called a "standard form," a classic solution, one that seems to be the very best, at least within the time.

5-11 A

5-11 A and B Usually there is a path of development from the inception of an idea through change, improvement, failure, and finally to what has been called its "standard form." The standard form is a plateau of development. This Anon chair of 1900 was a highly successful standard form for its combination of style, material, durability and general acceptance by the public. The laboratory jar is another standard form that has been unchanged for many years.

5-11 B

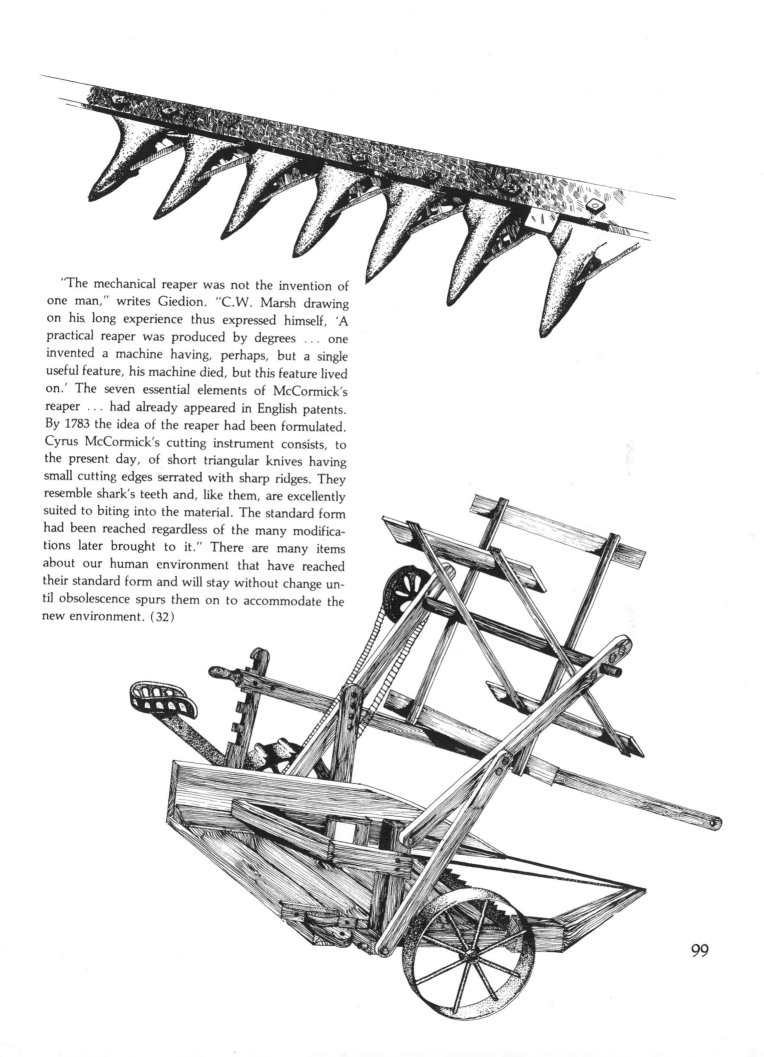

"The mechanical reaper was not the invention of one man," writes Giedion. "C.W. Marsh drawing on his long experience thus expressed himself, 'A practical reaper was produced by degrees ... one invented a machine having, perhaps, but a single useful feature, his machine died, but this feature lived on.' The seven essential elements of McCormick's reaper ... had already appeared in English patents. By 1783 the idea of the reaper had been formulated. Cyrus McCormick's cutting instrument consists, to the present day, of short triangular knives having small cutting edges serrated with sharp ridges. They resemble shark's teeth and, like them, are excellently suited to biting into the material. The standard form had been reached regardless of the many modifications later brought to it." There are many items about our human environment that have reached their standard form and will stay without change until obsolescence spurs them on to accommodate the new environment. (32)

99

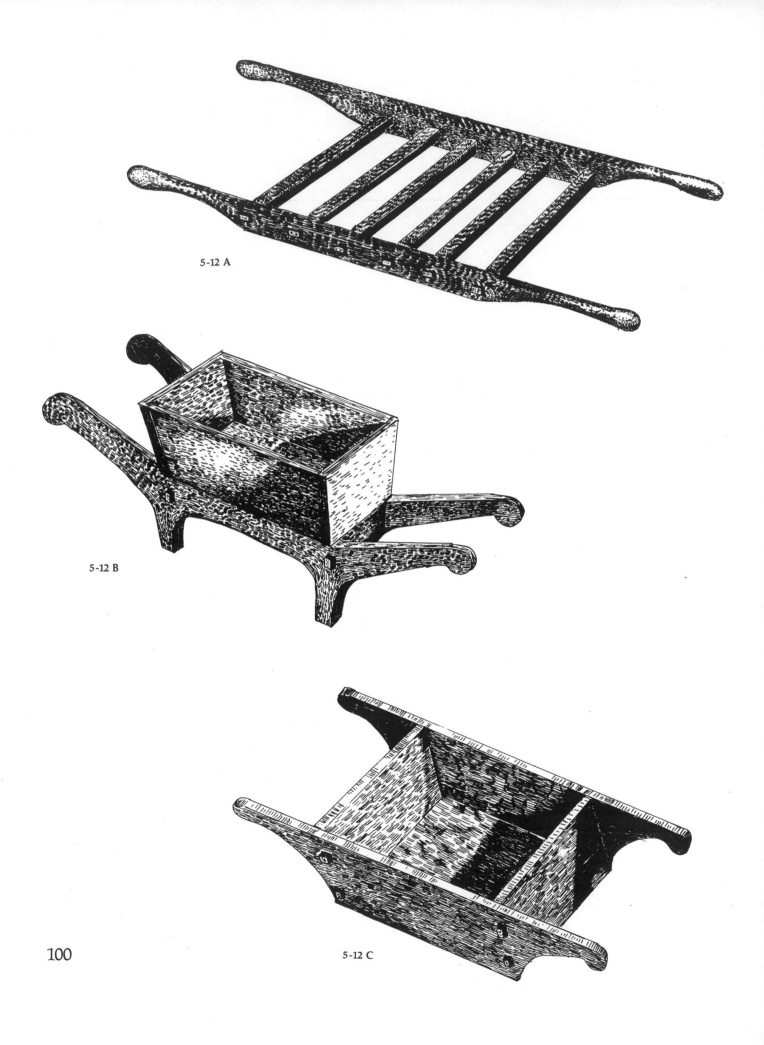

5-12 A

5-12 B

5-12 C

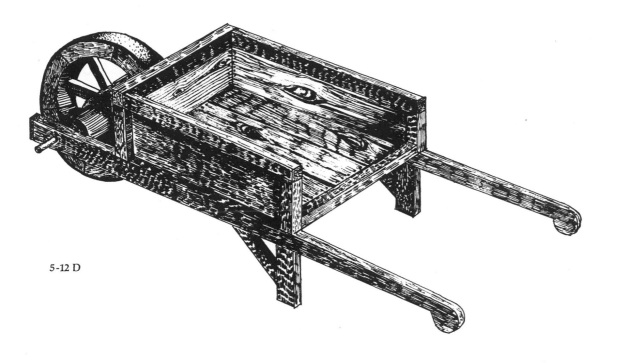

5-12 D

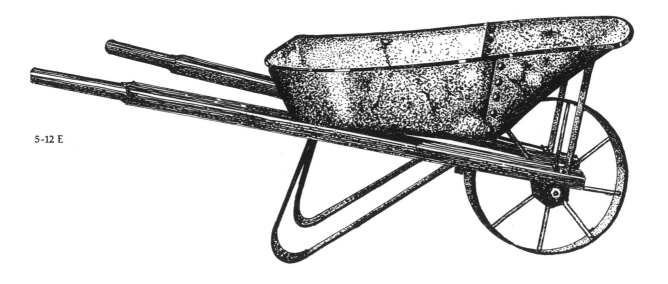

5-12 E

5-12 A, B, C, D, E The evolution of the wheelbarrow passed through five, maybe six, different steps to its standard form. The wheelbarrow began as a handbarrow. The handbarrow was a litter carried between two laborers and capable of bearing medium sized objects. For sand or other similar loose or fine material the box upon handles was evolved; the box and its handles became integrated into one form in the third step; the next departure came with the realization that one laborer could be replaced by a wheel on the front end, leaving the handles and stand on the back. In the fifth step the standard form was reached with an inclined base to offset the slope while being carried, and a switch in materials, from wood to metal. The last step to date (not depicted), which may or may not become a standard form, is the substitution for the wheel of a pneumatic sphere to allow stability on rough ground.

6 THE ECOPHENOTYPIC EFFECT
The Form in its Environment

On a canyon floor a young spruce tree grows awkward and sparse, its spindly trunk reaching about twelve feet in height. Two disproportionate limbs support the majority of its growth as they hang their greenery in the only available sunlight. The other branches are half dead among dense undergrowth. The tree's roots, though, are full and well developed in the rich, moist ground. On a rock ledge above the canyon another young spruce scarcely two feet in height, but having the same mother cone, displays its short and thick balanced branches. Where it grows there is no competition for space and sunlight; however, below the surface of the small pocket of stony earth in which it lives, the tree's roots are contorted and wedged into every crack and fissure in search of sparse nutrient and water.

Had these genetically similar trees been planted in optimal and identically controlled conditions they would have developed into a twin pair, reflecting the typical conical spruce form and spruce root system. The difference between these two trees is due to the ecophenotypic effect; the outcome of form is always compromised by the effects of the environment on the individual. (33)

An organism's form and life is controlled by the ecophenotypic effect from the disposition of the sun in the solar system to the exact chemical composition in a droplet of water. The immediate environment of every stalk of wheat in a field and barnacle on a rock is slightly different from all those that surround it. The availability of food, the shade, the swirls of the wave, the movements of the wind, the competition for space, and a million other factors vary from inch to inch. With mobile and far-ranging creatures like birds or humans, the ecophenotypic effect is even more compounded, for the environment with all its chance factors is in constant renewal.

6-1

The ecophenotypic effect also controls the form of the artifacts of mankind, as they are made and as they are used.

The sweater with the right stretches, the old pants with the easy comfort, the shoes that stretch and wrinkle to fit only one pair of feet, an overstuffed chair that seems to have taken on a shape that best suits only one sitter, the loose third porch step, the door that needs lifting on the handle before it swings open, the stairs that guide the climber through small worn pockets on the treads, the sticking closet door, the window that holds itself just open enough — these are the wonderful peculiarities of things that have been influenced by their environment and use.

6-1 Nature relies on the ecophenotypic effect to bring about variety in the world. Without it, if such would be possible, there would be monotonous repetition, for individuals of a species tend to be much the same. The environment in which they live brings about individuality. If the Monterey pines that grow upon this bluff had been planted in a controlled forest they would have been considerably more uniform in size, balance of foliage and general form. The differences in this more difficult and varying environment come about because of changes in soil conditions and composition, sunlight, wind, ground water, insects, and animals. Since the branches are subject to varying conditions, some survive and some do not. The general form of the tree is largely controlled by the success of its different branches.

In 1928 a developer constructed seven identical houses facing three streets and having adjoining back yards. The developer purchased seven of everything. It was apparent at the end of the first year after completion that gardeners bought only three houses; the other four had long grass and weed patches. By 1934 most needed repainting and two were vacant. All were occupied in 1940; two had converted garages; one had no garage at all. One had several twelve-year-old maples lining the drive. At the end of the forties one had had a fire and had been re-sided, one had been modernized with squared-off stucco, two round windows and a rounded entry. The fifties saw new roofs and driveways, disappearing porches, a family room, a guest cottage and a greenhouse.

By 1967 there was redwood siding, converted basements, fences, hedges, and several large trees. Today the observer would have had to spend some time to know that they were all the same house in 1928.

The process of manufacture is a continuum beginning with atomic structure, which becomes material substance to be shaped by natural processes of growth, accretion, and crystallization, and then manipulated by the human hand into artifacts. Further alteration is effected by time and use. The ecophenotypic effect is present at all these levels, though great effort is made to minimize variation in modern factory production.

As a direct human involvement in manufacture becomes less the level of error is lower, for the human hand lacks the precision necessary for accuracy in the repetitive production of goods. The less the involvement of the human hand in actual production, the greater is the chance for unchanging accuracy.

6-2 This block of row houses, a section of which is shown, was built in 1903. They were all built of the same materials in the same style. Expedience was the only reason for the duplication. It is cheaper, speedier, and far less trouble to construct them in the same way than to make them different. Though they have existed next to each other for all these years, each house's personal environment of people has been very different.

Through each door since 1903 the families have come and gone, each bringing to the house changes, some drastic, some hardly noticeable. Some people have put change on top of other changes, and some houses have been returned to their original decor, the added styles of later years removed.

The first house in the row had the original ashlar stone covered with stucco and readapted to a Victorian style. The second house was re-faced with brick and made into a Georgian mansion, of sorts. The third was unchanged until 1972, when it was covered with diagonal cedar siding, black window mullions and a floating stairway. The fourth went through several changes and finally was returned faithfully to its original state. The fifth was modernized in 1937 and has since become a period piece. The sixth has never had any systematic changes brought to it but has only been repaired with current items as parts gave out. The seventh house has never been changed at all.

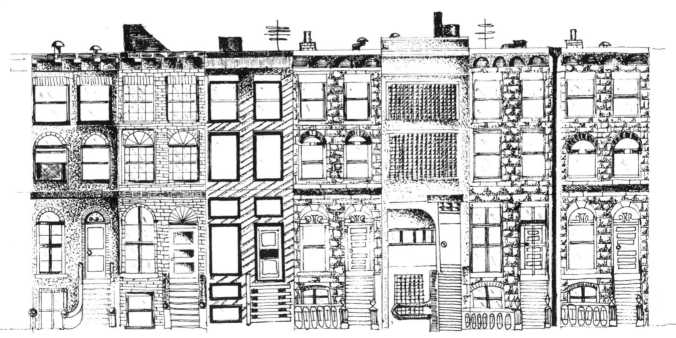

Siegfried Giedion writes:

"The human hand is a prehensile tool, a grasping instrument. It can seize, hold, press, mold with ease. It can search and feed. Flexibility and articulation are its key words. The triple-articulated fingers, the wrists, the elbow, the shoulders and on occasion, the trunk and legs heighten the flexibility and adaptability of the hand. Muscles and tendons determine how it will seize and hold objects. Its sensitive skin feels and recognizes materials. The eye steers its movements. But vital to all this integrated work is the mind that governs and feelings that lend it life. The kneading of bread; the folding of a cloth; the moving of brush over canvas; each movement has its roots in the mind. For all the complicated tasks to which this organic tool may be used, to one thing it is poorly suited: automation. In its very way of performing movement, the hand is ill-fitted to work with mathematical precision. Each movement depends on an order that the brain must constantly repeat. It wholly contradicts the organic, based on growth and change, to suffer automatization." (34)

Though mostly eliminated from manufacture today, hand production was once the only possibility and within the context of the eighteenth century workshop, inconsistency in form and design was not necessarily a question of the right way and the wrong way. Change from product to product was expected and even desired.

With a spokeshave a wagonwright trims a dozen wooden spokes to fit into the wheel that he is working to finish. It is his intent that each spoke will be as nearly as possible identical so that the wheel will run in true balance. Each of the wagon's four wheels should also be as similar as possible to offer equal alignment, ride, and service. And to maintain his reputation, the wagonwright attempts to make each wagon equally good to achieve a standard of excellence. But the wagonwright works with oak and elm, ash and wrought iron—excellent materials for the job, but materials filled with variation in hardness, grain, weight, stability and age at time of cut. The wagonwright uses hand tools, measures by thumb and eye, and assembles by reckoning; and the materials respond differently. Each spoke is not the same as the others, each wheel is assembled slightly differently upon axles that are longer or shorter, thicker or narrower, and are beneath wagon frames and beds with variation. The differences are small but important; they are not necessarily a matter of

good and not good. Rather, they are simply not the same. Variations are caused by environmental conditions during the growth of the tree, refinement of the iron, and forming and assembly of the wagon.

The wagonwright, with some help, will make four wagons a year. In three years twelve wagons will have left his shop. All are essentially the same by his and his customers' accounting.

When the wagons leave for their places of work they will again encounter the inconsistencies of human action. In five years, ten years, twenty years, the wagons that are still in service will be even more different from one another.

Before the industrial revolution many families, especially in the rural communities, had the obligation to make or grow the large majority of the goods they used: the clothing, the furniture, the food, tools, utensils, and the home itself. These people were generalists, good at many things but specialists at none. The things they produced were similar but not identical to artifacts made by their parents and neighbors. In these pre-industrial homes the ecophenotypic effect was the prevalent force: variety was manifest, not because of a conscious effort to make things different from one another, but through the basic inconsistencies in human beings.

As populations increased and settlements grew larger and closer together, the generalist gave way to the specialist. In the home craft society, inevitably, particular talents in individuals appeared. It might be that there was a family member who was able to make shoes better than anyone else, or a person with the instinct for working wood. Knowledge of these people spread in the communities and they were in demand for their services. These people ceased to be generalists, for they stopped doing other things to concentrate upon serving these demands. They were soon practiced and unquestionably superior at one thing, but narrower in their scope. With this specialization the artisans made their appearance.

The coopers, cobblers, blacksmiths, shipwrights, wagonwrights, wheelwrights, and coppersmiths delivered products with far greater accuracy and craftsmanship than the farmers working in their sheds. The ecophenotypic effect was reduced. The workplace was organized and the approach to work was more uniform. The artisans specialized in one material from which they made a large variety of goods, like the woodworkers or blacksmiths, or they specialized in the production of a single item, a boat or a wagon in which they used several materials. Special secret methods of the trade were established, which encouraged the separation of the crafts from the general society. By the time the craft guilds came into existence the production methods were thought of as the exclusive possession of the artisan.

When the artisan was called upon to make something of complexity, requiring several parts, each part was made separately from raw material and fitted individually to the adjacent parts. This process was continued until the parts were finished and assembled, whereupon the product was set aside to start anew. Each product with its component parts, though identical in function, was different from all those that preceded it and those that came after. The differences were slight variations in dimensions and even slighter changes in forms.

The craft of the artisans gained wide admiration for quality, but with a changing society quantity became increasingly more important, and the artisans' methods were not adequate for mass production for a mass society. When the artisan's product failed through a broken or worn part, the entire object would have to be returned to its maker for an exact fitting, for the parts, though similar from item to item, were not interchangeable due to the slight dif-

6-3 When most of the goods of the world were produced by artisans the variety of products was enormous. Each country boasted an approach to its own way of life; within the country each area had its own style; and within each area the towns and cities each had a specialty or group of artifacts for which it was known. Each individual artisan was proud of the fact that his approach was different from the others. And finally because of the artisans' hand-crafting techniques, each item that they produced over their lifetime of work had a personality of its own.

6-3

6-4

ferences in dimensioning. This produced inconvenience, and lost time. With more centralized production, the geographic distances between maker and user were increasing.

In the beginning, the artisan economy was based on one or two persons working collectively. Then apprentices and less skilled helpers were taken into the larger shops. They were given simple tasks like the preparation of raw materials, rough cutting, grinding, or polishing. Because of their lack of skill they could not follow the process through from start to finish as did the experienced artisans.

It became evident that each of the unskilled helpers could be taught just one of the many tasks the artisan performed in a short period of time. Thus, though many people would be replacing one, the work would be speeded considerably and the required skills would not have to be accumulated over half a lifetime. With this revolutionary thought came the birth of a new concept, division of labor. And specialization was again subdivided.

It took the great skill of the artisan locksmith to produce a mechanism of the intricacy and complexity

6-4 This cooper produces barrels, buckets, and drums. He makes each part himself, from the cutting of the barrel top (as shown), to the fashioning of the staves, to the assembling of the complete product. Every part of the operation is his responsibility and so he must know and have the skill to complete each task.

of a lock from raw material to the assembled individually finished and fitted parts. But a less skilled worker could be taught to make just one of those parts if he did nothing but produce that single part over and over again. However, the conditions in which the worker operated had to change considerably.

Let us say that a simple barn door lock was to be constructed and it had fifteen parts. Fifteen work stations would have to be built into the expanded artisan's shop, which had now become a manufactury. The artisans did not have time for handwork now, for they were busy directing the workers and overseeing the production level and consistency. The tools of production, meanwhile, had become larger and more sophisticated and were driven by an external power source: first wind and water, then steam power. (35)

Lest the workers make mistakes in dimensioning, each was provided with a template which would

107

6-5

guide the shaping and cutting operation. These templates were called jigs, and they contained all the information the workers needed to know about the making of the part that was their responsibility.

Guiding a tool to follow a jig was a simple assignment, but making that jig was much more difficult, and this became the new job of the artisan. In the past, the artisans carried all the knowledge about the design and dimensioning of their artifacts in their heads; nothing was written. Now they were in the position of transmitting that information. Accurate plans and drawings had to record the artisan's knowledge. The artisans became designers, creators of tools and jigs. With the use of recorded information on plans and jigs for repetitious accuracy, uniformity was increased and the ecophenotypic effect was decreased even more.

Accuracy and division of labor had to go together. If the fifteen locksmiths separately providing the fifteen parts for the barn door lock attempted to custom fit each part, there would be hopeless confusion. With jigs the parts could be made accurately enough

to allow any part to fit any assembly. The implications of this system would not only make production faster and smoother, but would reinforce the new centralized society. A farmer living two hundred miles away from the factory could order by mail a replacement part from the catalog, and know that the new part would correspond exactly with the part to be replaced.

The last step in the evolution of industrialization involved the assembly process. With the generalists and the artisans, the assembly operation had to be an integral part of component fabrication. With limited production in the small artisans' shops, the materials and parts were moved in to be assembled to the product. Line flow or assembly line production was just the opposite. (36)

At the assembly plant, the barn door lock will pick up its fifteen parts as it moves past the assemblers, a part or two at each assembly point. The assemblers remain stationary. This method organizes motion by requiring a set series of operations performed on each lock assembly as it passes. Again the training time is reduced and production speeded. The worker is now so specialized that a few simple repetitive actions account for an occupation. (37)

Human intervention in the production of goods is becoming steadily less frequent. The completion of a product from a raw to a finished state without the touch of a hand has been achieved. The intent and the goal of manufacture has been a pragmatic one; humans are unpredictable in disposition as well as

hand action. The line runs steadily and uniformly without people.

Achieved also was the transition from production of artifacts of greatly differing form and quality, made by unspecialized generalists for local or family members, to a highly controlled automated process of identical products with uniform components for a mass population. The transition was a logical one, and methods of production have kept abreast with demand, but only at the cost of individuality. With standardization and uniformity, random and intentional variation between products has been almost eliminated.

The industrialization of the late twentieth century may represent a rather crude solution to those who follow us. Doubtlessly there are many ways to regain the individuality, personal quality, and even consumer involvement in manufacture, while maintaining high quality and quantity.

With relatively simple modifications, it could be that instead of designers producing finished products they would design systems of interchangeable components for products. They could also design basic components to fit many different kinds of products. The purchaser would have an enormous number of options of complexity, cost, size, form, and degree of refinement of function, as well as quality and option

6-5 When production was translated to the factory from the artisan the responsibility of manufacture was subdivided. The factory workers needed only the skill and knowledge to make one part, or to perform even one step in the making of one part; this task they performed over and over. Their actions were guided by plans or jigs so variation and error from part to part were reduced to a minimum. Assembly of the parts occurred separately at another location.

6-6 In the very early 1800's, Henry Maudslay invented and patented a simple addition to the lathe (the lathe had been in use for thousands of years). This device was one of the most influential inventions of the 19th century. Up to this point all lathe cutting was brought about by the human hand holding the cutting tool against the work. Maudslay's device was called a slide rest (in the center of the lathe pictured). The slide rest carried the cutting tool to the work and held it firmly. This lathe of Maudslay's was capable of producing parts with accuracy to the thousandth of an inch. Tools such as this produced not parts of products but parts of other tools, so that though this tool was made by hand it was capable of making tools that had an accuracy impossible to achieve by hand.

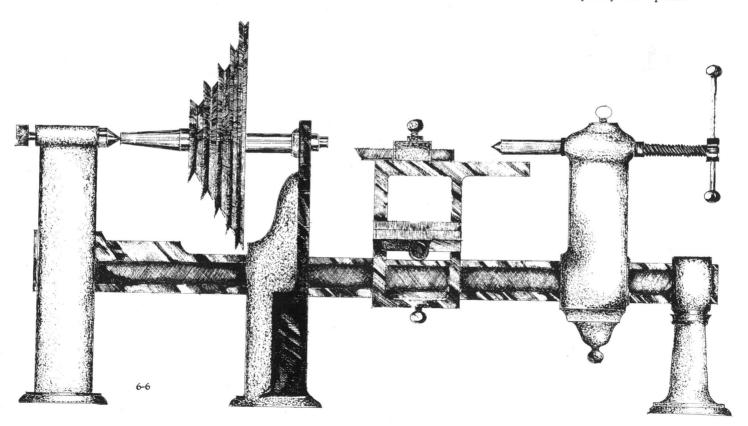

6-6

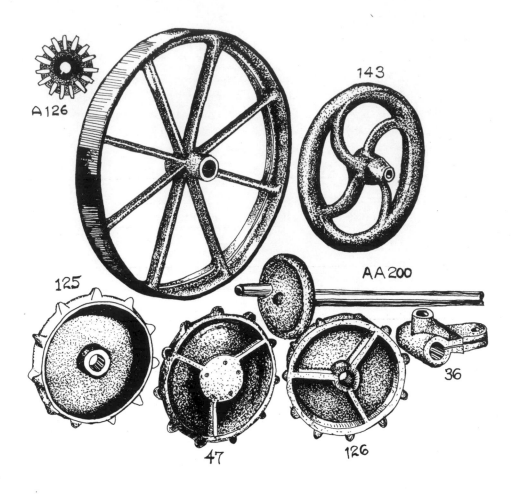

6-7

of degree of involvement. The general populace would be enticed back into the role of involved generalist (by cost reduction, increase of option, and control of quality), and again people would be able to exert an influence on their personal environment. (39)

What is the value of the ecophenotypic effect to those who design and build, and those who use these products? If the product is designed to improve with use, the designer must be totally aware of the product's intended environment, which is only rarely possible. The larger factors can be researched through market analysis, but to gear a product to individual personal markets is only possible by having the user effect the final stages of the design.

Is it possible to build the improvement factor into the product? We are aware of some of the simpler improvements brought about by users. Shoes are never less comfortable than the day they are carried from the store; a smoker's pipe wears into its task and continues improving over years; a catcher's mitt pockets better after use. Landscaping must wait to fulfill its promise and improve with age as do wines, cheeses, and many tools.

Much of natural design is conceived with an improvement factor. Living materials often fare better

6-7 This drawing is taken from part of a page of Walter Wood's agricultural implement catalogue of 1867. Through the use of the modern concept of interchangeability of parts and this catalogue, the farmer could send for a replacement part rather that requiring the local blacksmith to hand build or repair the broken part.

6-8 A and B. It is interesting to examine the relationship of animal and plant material to inorganic material in the context of wear and stress. Metal and stone diminish in volume and lose their surfaces when subjected to abrasion, erosion, and rubbing. But these actions stimulate biological systems, which spurs cell growth, and so builds proportionately more material where it is needed. The wearing process is compensated.

The same kind of correction process is found in stress. Fruit trees thicken and strengthen limbs and twigs as their fruit gathers weight. The above illustration of an ox scapula bone is a dramatic example of stress compensation in animals. Bone is not only a living, but a highly plastic structure. The bone's structure is formed of small fibers called trabeculae. These trabeculae are in a constant state of removal and addition. When the new are added they are placed exactly parallel with the stress on the bone. The cracks in the old ox bone that this drawing was copied from follow complex paths of the trabeculae as the last demands of the animal in old age. The trabeculae form a perfect stress pattern of the bone. The analogy in this illustration to the illustration of wood #1-14 and iron #1-15 should be noted.

in their reactions to stress and abrasion than do the materials of the non-living and inorganic. When faced with heavy use, the soles of our shoes grow thin but the soles of our feet grow thick. Animal tissue and bone are capable of repairing and replacing themselves constantly. (38)

Animal bone is not permanent during life, but is in a continual process of removal (osteoclast), and addition (osteoblast). As the forces and loads on the bone shift through maturity, increased weight and change in activity over a period of time, or posture change through age or accident, the bone gradually realigns itself to respond to load shifts; the grain of the bone "stretches" up to meet its force. The bone is always making itself best suited for a changing load situation. Structures of mankind, however, must be built for maximum load at all times whether in demand or not.

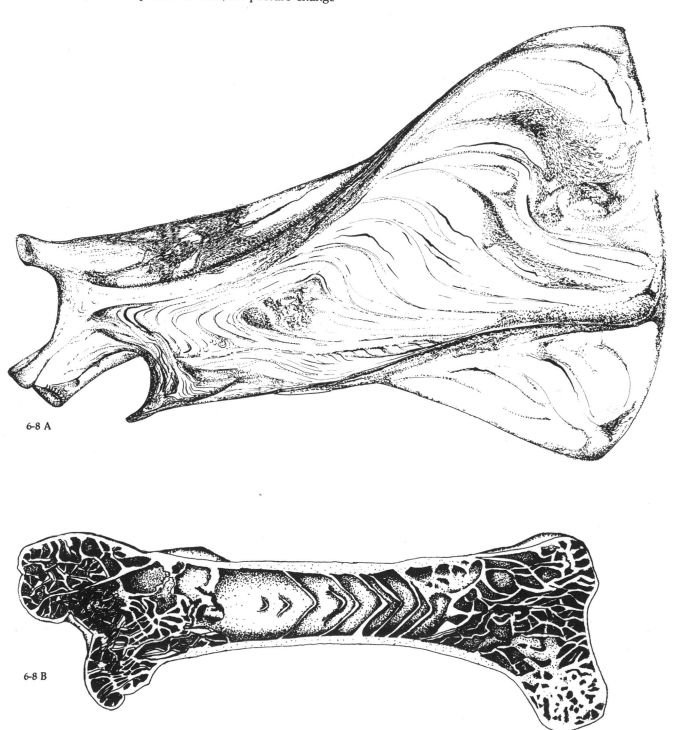

6-8 A

6-8 B

As a more complex example of environmentally improved human design, consider the following. A leading architect once built a cluster of large office buildings set in a central green. When construction was completed, the landscape crew went to the architect for his word on placement of the sidewalk grid between the buildings. "Not yet," was the architect's reply, "just plant the grass solidly between the buildings." This was done, and by late summer the new lawn was laced with pathways of trodden grass, connecting building to building, and building to the outside. The paths followed the most efficient line between the points of connection, turned in easy curves rather than right angles, and were sized according to traffic flow. In the fall the architect simply paved in the pathways. Not only did the pathways have a design beauty, but they responded directly to user needs. Furthermore, there was never any need to put up "DON'T WALK ON THE GRASS" signs, for there was always just the right little shortcut path.

If change through use, wear, and repair is unavoidable, it is certainly satisfying to find that the change itself is an improvement; that the product grows better rather than poorer as it ages, and wears in instead of wearing out.

6-9 Though these boots started identically to tens of thousands of others, they became slightly more individual every day they were worn, until they were pushed, crinkled, bent, and stretched to exactly as possible correspond to the feet to which they very much belong. It might be fair to say that shoes don't wear out as much as in.

6-9

7 TELEOLOGY
A World Unity

Children learning about the world are not afraid to ask about the wind and the water, the cloud and the mountain in one breath. In subtle ignorance, their questions come from an overview. Slowly they begin to perceive an order to life, a logic barely understood but felt to exist. Then, when the investigation is just finding reward, it is dropped and left entirely because childhood has passed.

If the way is picked up again when the child becomes an adult in one of the sciences the investigation will become an inner view, one of specialization, learning thoroughly the intricacies of the parts of but one aspect of one branch of science; for the modern view has been concerned with examining the pieces to find their relationship to the whole. It is thought that by this method of part by part accumulation a picture will begin to take form which will in turn fit into an even greater scheme, and on, and on.

The word teleology comes from the Greek teleos — the final cause. Teleology is the philosophy and belief that all in the world and beyond is interconnected and there is an overriding cause above and beyond the immediate cause.

A volcano erupts from a cornfield and makes a mountain where there was none before. The immediate cause was the venting of pressured gas and magma but the form of the cone, flow of the lava, the spread of the debris, the forms of cooling, shrinking, and cracking in the new rock are all predetermined and can all be anticipated, for they are responding to a set of laws that govern, and have governed, the world and the universe since it began.

The ancient Greeks, like children, began the study of science with an overview. They looked at the world about them to find laws that showed a relationship between the pieces. They believed that the basic laws of nature prevail over all that is put together by nature or man; a lyre in tune, the work of a craftsman, a cactus or a seashell. If the modern world were to consider teleology in its own terms, it might be said that all substance about us has the same physiochemical basis. Animal fur and bone, shell and plastic membrane and soap film, are all particles of matter moulded by the same physical laws.

The Greek's Final Cause is the overview; the modern innerview, that knowledge accumulates piece by piece, is the immediate cause. They cannot be taken separately, but must be blended to give the picture of all that has been done, and all that is possible in the form and structure of organic and inorganic, animate and inanimate things. The innerview has been relentlessly pursued by modern science, but few have attempted the more subtle, but precarious path of finding the correlations between diversities.

The "search for relationships between things apparently disconnected" is known as the Aristotelian

113

Quest. A few giants among men have emerged through the years, since the Greeks, who have taken up this quest. Leonardo da Vinci was among them. As a sculptor, architect, engineer, anatomist, and naturalist, he quested for an order in life.

Da Vinci's observations led him to be the first to note what has since become known as phyllotaxy, or leaf arrangement. In examining an elm tree, he wrote, "...the leaves are so distributed on the plant, so that one shall cover the other as little as possible, but shall lie alternately one above the other..." Galileo, among so much else, determined the Principles of Similitude in which he mathematically showed that as structures, living or not, increase in size, they become disproportionately heavy, so that the very large, elephants and warships, must be grown or built in a much sturdier fashion than the small.

In the year that Galileo died, 1642, Isaac Newton was born. Through simple observations, Newton developed his Principles of Motion, which led him to examine the movement of the heavens, an overview to the extreme. One of the greatest teleologists was D'Arcy Thompson. Thompson was born in the last century and worked well into this one. His work took him into all aspects of morphology, the science of form. In his own words, he reminds us, "it behooves us always to remember ... it has taken great men to discover simple things. They are very great names indeed which we couple with the explanations of the path of a stone, the droop of a chain, the tints of a bubble, the shadows in a cup." (40)

D'Arcy Thompson studied all aspects of the living and inanimate world. From his vantage point, the tree is not only one of a family or genus, but a living entity made up of cells that respond to the same earthly laws to which all else responds. In Thompson's view, the tree owes its every curve and outline to the material from which it is made, and the relentless pull of gravity. The angle of its intersection limbs forms a profile that resembles a logarithmic curve. This gives it equal strength throughout. The leaf placement is according to a preset Fibonacci series. The tree's maximum height is determined by the laws of similitude. Its whole form is a diagram of the forces placed against it.

The silhouette of a two-hundred-year-old oak outlined against the winter sky is reminiscent of a river and its tributaries seen from above, and this is not so strange if one thinks of the river and the oak as being flow lines that connect one to many. The thousands of leaves of the oak are brought into contact at one point on the ground through the trunk, and the river pulls hundreds of thousands of water sources into its stream and ultimately pushes them out through its mouth.

When comparing the forms of totally alien organisms and substances, we must remain somewhat vague because of the immense number of physical laws governing the outcome of a complicated form. We can determine some of the obvious ones and only guess at the others. Added to this is the fact that the course of development of an invidual is subjected to deformation: all human faces are different; all squirrels and mountains are different. Teleology deals with related forms, rather than a precise definition of each individual. Mathematically we can define the form of a wave or a heap of sand, but as Thompson has pointed out, never ask a mathematician to define the form of any particular wave of the sea, nor the actual form of any mountain peak or hill.

About eight hundred years ago a dreamy, brilliant boy was born to an Italian customs official. His family gave him the name Leonardo, but the town gave him many other mildly chiding names: "The Blockhead," and to include his father, "Son of the Simpleton," Fibonacci. This name followed him through history. While still young, Fibonacci wrote a treatise on the Arabic numeral. His manuscript was largely responsible for the introduction of the new letter form into Europe. Almost hidden on the back pages of this publication was a little mathematical puzzle that presented a question and posed a solution to one of the greatest natural intrigues in history. Like grasping another source of life, Fibonacci with this simple riddle caught a glimpse into a universal truth that still remains only partially solved. Fibonacci asked the deceptively easy question: how many rabbits would result from one pair in one year if A) every month each pair of rabbits produced another pair, with the exception that B) each new pair started to produce on the second month following their own birth.

7-1 A and B Both the stem and branches of plants, and such things as a spruce cone, show the spiral patterns typical of all plant growth. The scales on the cone can be seen to spiral up to the right and left. This Norway spruce cone has 13 scales in the left rotating spiral and 21 in the right rotating spiral. These are two figures in the Fibonacci series. Often sub-species are identified by their scale count.

114

Fibonacci answered his own question as follows: the first month nothing happened, for the original pair was too young.

Month one = 1 pair

The second month the second pair was born.

Month two = 2 pair

In the third month only the original pair produced.

Month three = 3 pair

But the fourth month both the original pair and the first born pair, which was of age now, produced.

Month four = 5 pair

The fifth month the original pair produced, plus the first born and the second born, so three new pairs were added.

Month five = 8 pair

And so on to twelve:

Month six = 13 pair
Month seven = 21 pair

Month eight = 34 pair
Month nine = 55 pair
Month ten = 89 pair
Month eleven = 144 pair
Month twelve = 233 pair

For his purposes in the puzzle Fibonacci stopped at twelve, though the series could be carried on ad infinitum. Whether he discovered it before or afterwards, Fibonacci had formulated perhaps one of the most significant series of numbers ever assembled.

Though appearing almost random at first glance it will soon be noted that each number in turn is the sum of the two just preceding it:

$$5 + 8 = 13$$
$$8 + 13 = 21$$
$$13 + 21 = 34$$
$$21 + 34 = 55$$
$$34 + 55 = 89$$

or higher up in the series

$$4181 + 6765 = 10,946$$

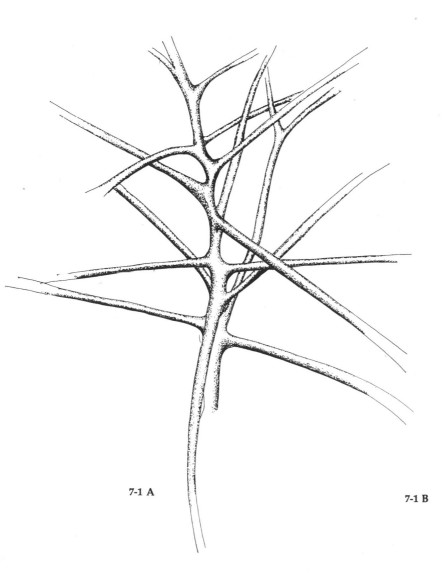

7-1 A

7-1 B

To make connections to the Fibonacci series we must go back a bit. As noted by Leonardo da Vinci, the leaves of a tree (or other leafy plant) cover one another as little as possible so as to expose each to a maximum amount of sunlight. The same applies to the placement of branches upon the trunk. Through infinite experimentation, failure and success, natural systems have evolved a pattern of spiral growth as the best method of leaf arrangement to allow this exposure. The leaves follow a winding path as they develop on the newly formed stem, one ahead of and slightly rotated about the stem from the one preceding it. There are many variations of density in the number of leaves and tightness of spiral, but there is always a numerical relationship to the Fibonacci series.

A certain plant may have 13 leaves in 8 turns around the stalk, or 13 leaves in 5 turns, or a plant may have a total of 5 spirals in one direction and 13 in the opposite direction. The same occurrence can be found in all sorts of vegetable growth: scales in a pine cone, branches of a tree, thorns on a bush, or seeds in

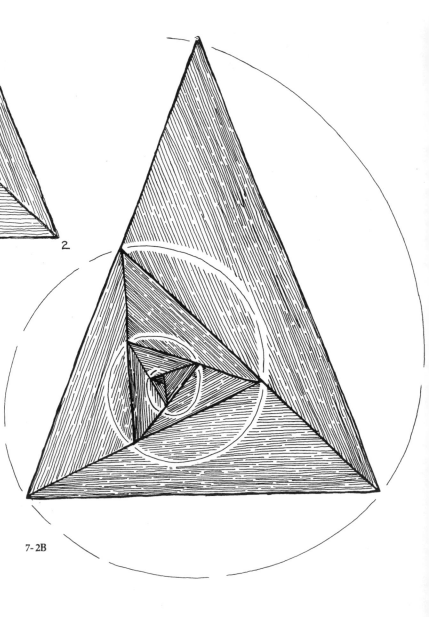

7-2B

a sunflower which might have 89 rows of seeds spiraling out from the center in one direction and 144 in the opposite direction. All these numbers are in the Fibonacci series.

A spiral is a curving line that increases its radius as it circles its central pole (the closed circle has a constant radius). The rate of radial increase determines the type of spiral. Above all others one spiral is dominant in nature. It is known by several names: the logarithmic spiral, the equiangular spiral, and sometimes the spiral of the golden mean. It is defined as a spiral in which each new increment along the curve is proportional to the distance from the central pole (the radius), or the distance already traversed along the spiral. A radius intersecting the spiral at any point always crosses it at the same angle.

These curious facts give hints of the very special nature of the equiangular spiral and give reason to its repeated use in nature. As D'Arcy Thompson has pointed out, a child grows into an adult by adding some growth to every part of the body, thus roughly maintaining the same form. The human body grows up and old all together; the body is approximately all the same age. The seashell and related forms grow from one point only, the edge around the opening of the shell (called the generating circle). But the equiangular spiral shell is able to maintain the exact proportions in the immature and the adult forms. The material of an adult shell represents parts that were laid down when the snail was beginning life, as well as the most recent growth; so the seashell is aged at the center and young at the largest forward edge. No matter how large it becomes, the equiangular spiral never changes its proportion. (41)

7-2 A and B The large figure above is an isosceles triangle — points 1, 2, 3. If the base of this triangle — 2, 3 is rotated up to the side, another isosceles triangle is formed—2,3,4, and if the base of that triangle is again rotated, a still smaller isosceles triangle is formed — 3,4,5 and so on — 4,5,6 — 5,6,7 — 6,7,8 — 7,8,9 — and 8,9,10. These points taken in a series become the tangents for an equiangular spiral.

7-3 Shells add new growth from the open end only, and in so doing increase their size while maintaining their exact proportions. The small drawing is a cross section of the shell showing the equiangular growth spiral of the shell.

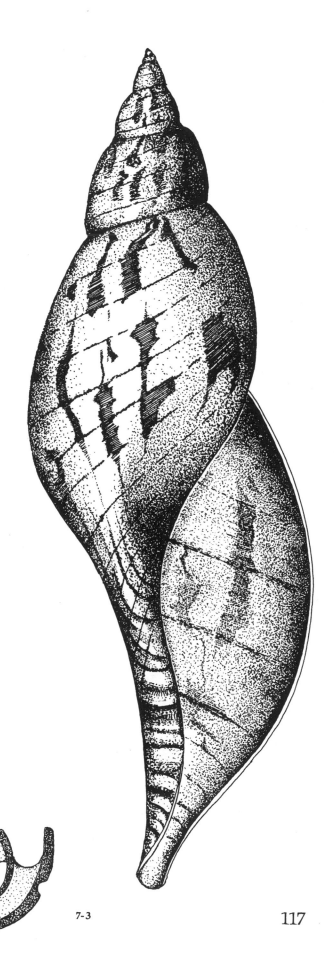

7-3

Horns, teeth, claws, beaks and tusks all grow this same way and exhibit the characteristics of the equiangular spiral, and all growth is from one point only.

Any radii cutting the equiangular spiral into sections of curves always divide the spiral into the same proportions as the radial lines cross concentric curves, and that proportion is always 1 to 0.618034.

I now ask the reader who is uncomfortable with mathematics to please bear with these figures, for they are important to the point (see accompanying drawing for clarification).

We now come back to the Fibonacci series with more interest, for we find that if any two consecutive numbers in the series are divided, larger into smaller, the number 0.6180 appears.

$$233 \overline{)\ 144} \quad 0.618025$$

$$610 \overline{)\ 377} \quad 0.618032$$

$$10946 \overline{)6965} \quad 0.6180339$$

The larger the numbers in the series, the closer to the ideal 0.618034 — try it!

This number 0.618034, derived from the Fibonacci series, forms a bridge between products of the human hand, eye and mind on the one hand, and natural design on the other.

Through graphic means and a precise and demanding eye the Greeks arrived at what they determined to be the perfect proportion. It is defined as follows: A line that is divided into two parts in such a way that the smaller part is in proportion to the larger part as the larger part is to the whole line. The dividing point was called the golden mean. The Greeks applied this proportioning to architecture, drawing, furniture, and objects of utility. One of the most elegant applications was to the rectangle, referred to as the rectangle of the divine section, or the golden rectangle. It was probable that the Greeks did *not* have the mathematical bridge between their proportions and the natural systems. For hundreds of centuries the Greeks' golden mean was known, forgotten, and found again, but it was probably never associated with the mathematics of nature until the seventh century A.D.

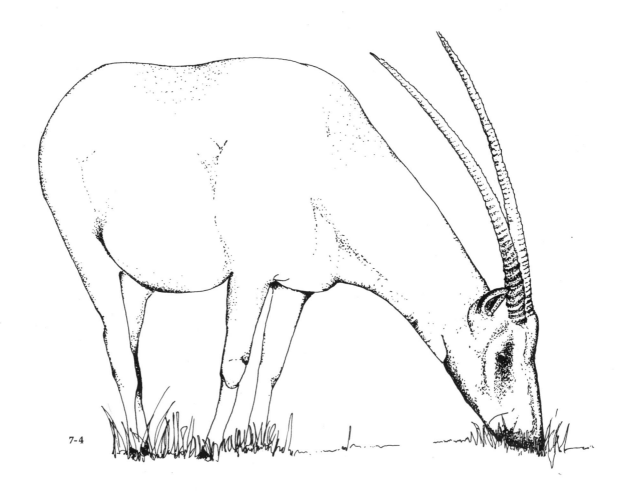

7-4

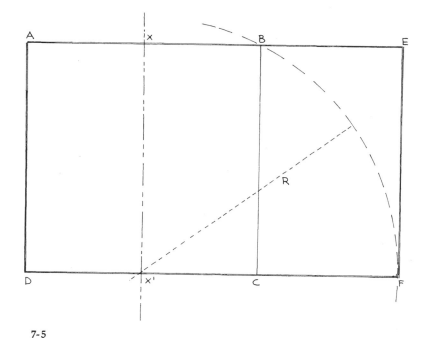

7-5

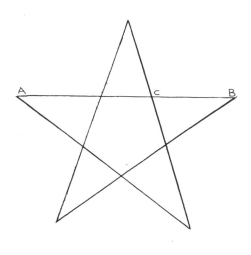

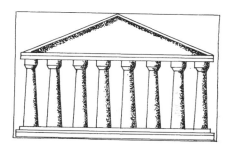

7-4 The horns of all horned animals are curved in equiangular spirals. Some are tight and compact curves like the mountain goat horn and some are like the gemsbok's four-foot-long gently curving horns.

7-5 Though it can be constructed mathematically it is probable that the Greeks discovered and used the golden rectangle only through the geometric formula.

The golden rectangle begins with a square (A,B,C,D). The square is divided in half (X,X₁). An arc is then struck through a diagonal corner (B) using an intersecting point of the bisecting line (X₁) as the center point of the arc, with the radial line (R) continued to bring the arc to intersect with an extension of the side of the square (DC). A new line is formed (DF), which is the side of the golden rectangle (A,E,F,D,), and also forms a smaller golden rectangle (B,E,F,C).

Mathematically AD to DF is a ratio of 1 to 1.61. It has also been found that other forms such as the five pointed star, or the pentacle, exhibit the same ratio. Line AC to AB is a ratio of 1 to 1.61.

The Greeks gave the Parthenon at Athens, as they did other forms, the proportions of the golden rectangle.

It must have been a terribly exciting moment for Jacob Bernoulli at his home in Basel in the late sixteen hundreds when he saw the first hint that the golden mean was connected with the Fibonacci series. With the flush of those rare moments of startling discovery he stepped off the sides of a golden rectangle and found them to be in an exact proportion of one to 0.618034.

The Greeks based all their serious works on some form of the golden mean. Their columns and statuary were constructed with golden proportions. The face of the Parthenon was built to the exact golden rectangle. The Greek vases fit within a golden rectangle and the human figure was divided into golden means.

Today there can be found exponents of the golden mean who will claim its association with rectangles found in modern forms as well as the proportions of ancient Egyptian pyramids and distant whirling spiral galaxies. These connections may indeed be there, but one must be cautious, for these "universal truths" are often so extraordinary that they entice the faithful to push into realms where that law does not belong; for nature does work in many strange ways, not just one.

The evolution of all things animate or inanimate takes place within a sea of forces. Some of these forces are dominant, some are scarcely there at all, but all exert some influence on the changing form. The force might be a necessity for placement of leaves to maximize sunlight or it might be a compression of space, a surface stress, heat, infusion with another substance, vibration, or sonic disturbance,

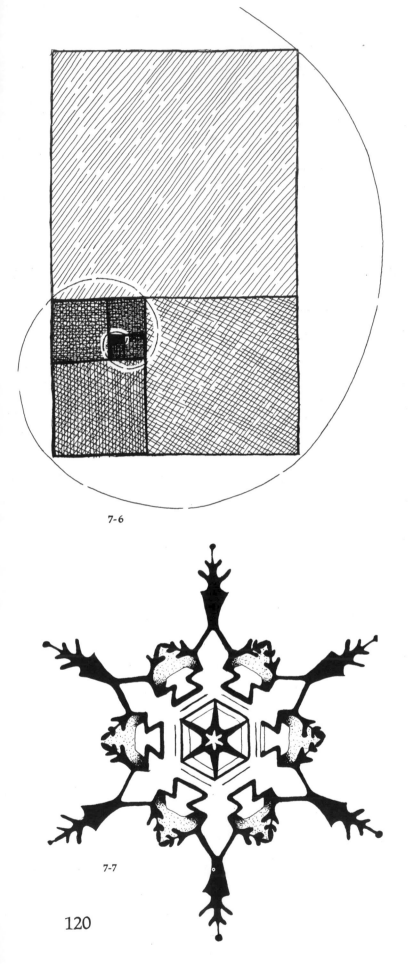

7-6

wind, torsion, electrical charge, gravitational pull, or any number and combination of other mechanical or chemical forces. The substance can only respond and its evolving form is a reflection of the forces, like a patch of froth on a slowly winding river revealing the currents and countercurrents. When the forces are complex and constantly shifting, the developing form is unpredictable, like an old pear tree that has been broken, pruned, and buffeted by the elements, or the skin of an aged elephant. But when the forces are more constant and predictable the forms evolve into rhythm, pattern, and symmetry. (42)

Symmetry in form reveals consistency of force. Radiate symmetry, the least complex, comes about from a single force having near total dominance on the development of the form. It is expressed on a two dimensional surface pattern in snowflakes, flowers, or the circling rings caused by the splash of a pebble on the surface of a still pond. Radiate symmetry in three-dimensional expressions are spherical forms. When two balanced forces a given distance apart exert equal influence upon a substance, a bi-polar form becomes evident. The two classic examples of this are the dividing cell and the poles of a magnet acting on metal filings. Bilateral symmetry is a more complicated force system. It results from forces expressed along a line. The higher forms of life are bilaterally symmetrical. The human body is the prime example. A form symmetrically proportioned about a central

7-6 When a golden rectangle is constructed with a square introduced into the end, another smaller golden rectangle results; if that in turn is divided with another square, still another smaller golden rectangle is formed. This process can continue on to the infinitely small as well as infinitely large rectangles. As with the isosceles triangle, if the points are used as tangents an equiangular spiral can be formed.

7-7 The snowflake is an example of radial symmetry. The form is organized about a central point.

7-8 A and B Another kind of symmetry is one which is organized about two poles. This is called bipolar symmetry. The action of two poles of a magnet upon metal filings on a sheet of paper shows very clearly the pattern of the field of force between the poles. The fields radiate in all directions from each pole but are strongest in the area between the poles. At the centerline is a point of equilibrium, a balance between the forces. Some metal filings accumulate here in a ridge, this called the equatorial plate.

The second drawing is of the approach to the metaphase of human cell division. Lined up in the center are the chromosomes. The poles are called asters; they separate each chromosome and divide them up and pull the cell apart. The small drawing below shows a cross-section of the entire cell having passed the metaphase, divided the chromosomes, and starting to split into two daughter cells.

7-7

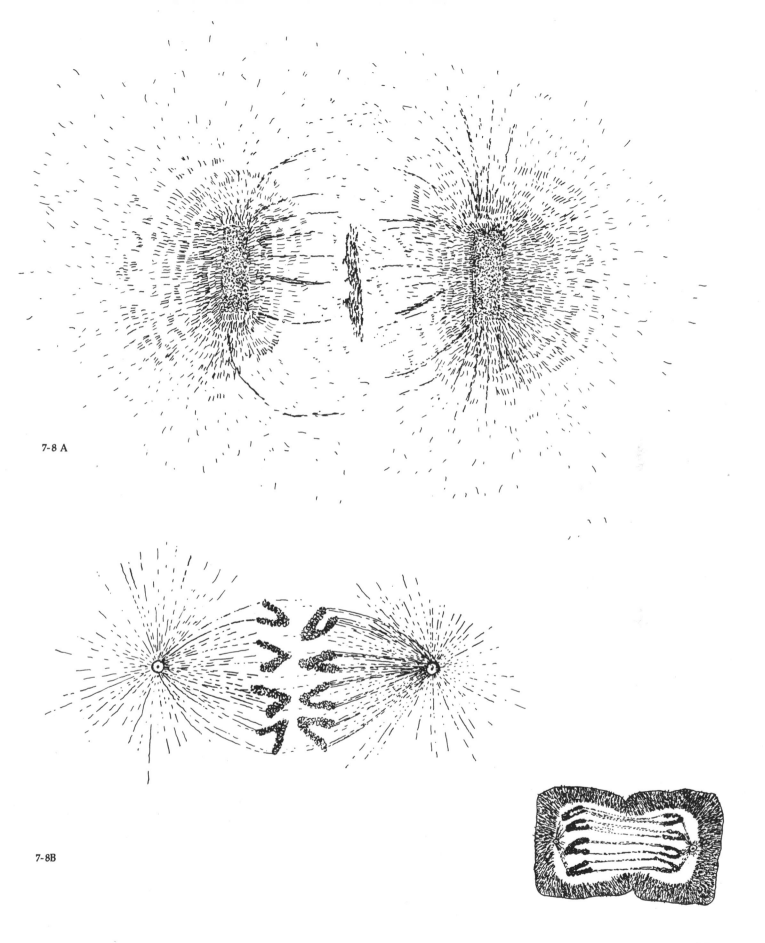

7-8 A

7-8B

121

7-9

line vertically circling the torso, the left and right are mirror reflections of each other. More complicated symmetry is found in patterns like bees' combs. Each bee in the process of producing a cell is a force within a field of force. Probably the most complex symmetry is the symmetry of the crystal. Crystallography is the three dimensional expression of a force system, very complex but highly structured and in dynamic balance. The human building analogy to the crystalline structure is the space lattice.

In all dynamic systems a host of forces are set against one another in combative control; equilibrium is the goal. In its bloom of life, a tree will raise tons of wood against gravity, only to fall back to earth again in death and decay. A dish of heated water produces complex patterns of diffusion that will disappear when the temperature becomes uniform and equilibrium is achieved.

A river strives toward equilibrium by transporting high water to the lowest possible place. The branching structure of a river is expressive of the lines of force upon which transportation and equalization takes place. If one thinks of these lines of force as avenues of energy and material transfer, a great number of similarities of form can be observed in a wide range of living and non-living objects. Bushes and trees are expressive of lines of force connecting one point to many points. The cross-section of a tomato

7-9 Most higher animals are organized about a central line that runs through the body laterally. This is called bilateral symmetry. The left and the right side are mirror reversals of each other, formed on each side of this line.

7-10 A, B, C. Above is the hind quarter of a Rhodesian Ridgeback dog. Where one alignment of fur meets another a vortex is formed. The vortex can be found in similar situations in the three states of matter: gases, liquids, and solids. It can be seen under the microscope behind moving microbes, in the swirls left by a boat oar, on a planetary weather map where streams of warm and cool air meet, or in the cross-section of a mushroom.

cut to reveal the internal intersection of stalk and fruit, the root pattern of kelp, and even the dispersion of ink in a container of water, are lines of force.

The manifestation of these lines of force often cuts through the boundaries between gases, liquids and solids. As an outrushing wave surges back into the sea, the moving stream of water clefts to each side and eddies back into itself, producing a vortex to the left and right. Smoke blown into the air shows the same kind of vortices, as it swirls out in an attempt to disperse. The alignment of fur on an animal's back and haunches is akin to liquid movement, as it flows in even lines over the body surface. When two or more flow lines moving in opposite directions encounter one another, there is often a vortex.

If a small drop of water is let fall into dry fine sand, a crater is left where the water splashed the grains of sand out with it. As it bounced off the ground, its ac-

122

7-10 A

7-10 B

7-10 C

123

tion was like a small explosion. The impact of the water hitting the sand threw out both water and sand from the center of impact. A steel jacketed bullet slamming into a steel plate will produce the same splash form. The craters on the moon are also splash forms. The fact that these craters are hundreds of thousands of times larger than the crater produced by the water in the sand, that they were made by the impact of one solid material against another, in a totally different environment two hundred and fifty-three thousand miles away, has little effect on the resulting form.

When the lines of force are moving past an object in a single direction the object usually responds in its development to these "stream lines."

A raindrop is such a stream formed body. The leading edge carries the bulk of fluid, holding partly to its spherical form. The trailing edge is drawn out by the streamlines moving past it. The raindrop, in other words, attempts to compromise its own spherical form with the stream of air moving swiftly past. The smaller raindrops are more spherical because they compromise less to the stream formation, held closer to a sphere by their proportionally greater surface tension.

An egg is formed inside the body of the bird as a fairly uniform sphere, because the pressures are equal on all sides. The egg shell does not harden until it begins its travel down the oviduct. The pulsing of peristaltic contraction slowly moves the egg on its journey through the canal and also smoothes the spherical egg into its ovoid form. The egg comes out blunt end first, a streamline formed body. The yolk of a hard boiled egg can be seen to remain formed in its original sphere, for it was protected from stream formation by shell and albumen.

When a soft clay or sand shoreline erodes to the sea, the more durable rocks remain as headlands to

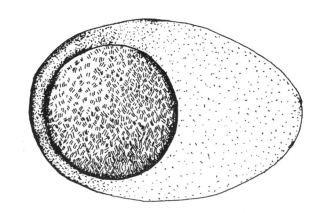

face the waves. These outcroppings often become separated islands, but if they lie close to a shore, a sand bar is often established on their lee quarter, serving as a connection between the headland and the shore. This formation is called a tombolo. The island fortress in France, Mont Saint-Michel, with its connecting spit of land, is a tombolo, The headland projects into the sea to receive the storm's impact which breaks on the leading edges, and flows in diminished force around the headland to meet the trailing bar on both sides, and there deposits its debris. When the wind is on-shore, the tombolo in effect is moving into the stream and the waves form themselves about the projecting land. The pattern of these streamlines can be seen from the air; the tombolo is a stream formed body.

Stream formations are found everywhere about us, as wind passes over a sand beach or snow, or moves clouds around a mountain top, as water passes over a tidal flat or out a garden hose.

Heinrich Hertel, in his book *Structure, Form and Movement* has said, "Bodily shape and way of life of a swimmer are adapted one to the other, hence by no means are all fish fast swimmers. It is obvious that the body of the walking fish cannot and need not be adopted for rapid swimming," but the bodies of the powerful swimmers are shaped to the "optimum solution from the point of view of hydrodynamics and propulsion." Through evolutionary means the physical properties of moving water form the body of the fish. (43)

7-11 The isle of Mont-Saint-Michel with its 750-year-old Gothic abbey lies off the Norman coast of France. Over millions of years the elements have cut into the shore, leaving behind an outcropping of rock. Its form is reflective of the streams of ocean and the power of the wind moving past it. The sand spit that connects it to the mainland trails behind like the tail of a meteor.

7-11

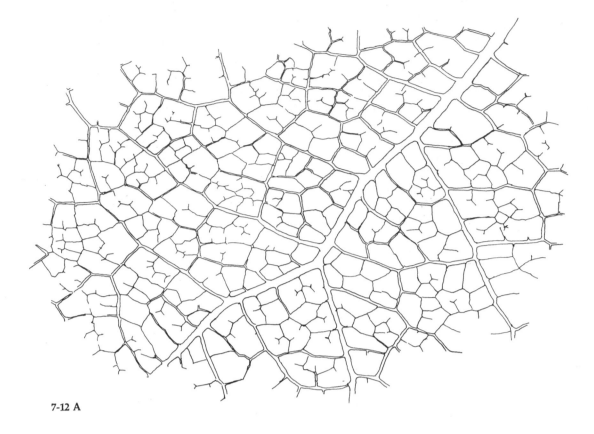

7-12 A

One of the most important forces in nature is the way in which space is divided. Nature abhors an undisturbed space, flat plane, and a vacuum. These she tries to fill with whatever is most convenient and expedient. As a result, a complete science has grown about the study of the methods she uses in the divisions and partitions of space. Her methods have far-reaching implications for human technology.

Observe, sometime, the cracks in a cement sidewalk or a macadam street, the checking of an old painting, or a cracking plaster wall, a parched riverway, or the splitting lines of a once wet, now dry plane of mud. Pick a maple leaf and hold it to the light to see the veinwork within, examine the cross-section of a bubble froth, and the clefting of a granite rock. All these phenomena, and thousands like them, fall under the unifying principle of what might be called space partitioning. For the moment, let's disregard size and material, whether we are speaking of living or non-living, organic or inorganic, and only concern ourselves with the abstract notion of a larger space that must be divided into smaller subdivisions, whether coming together, or being riven apart.

Surface tension is sometimes called surface energy, which it is indeed. When organic material is in the formation process, it is in a semi-liquid state, and so when leaf veins and arterial connections are laid down, they are subject to the laws of surface tension.

7-12 A, B, C. There are some clearly defined patterns nature uses in partitioning space (see text). These three drawings show the divisions of space in three situations. One drawing is a section of a maple leaf with its veins; the second drawing is a section of a dragonfly wing; and the third shows cracks in a mud bank. In all three situations the same forms occur in the intersections of these partition lines: where lines of equal size join they join at equal angles and form a three-way intersection; this is an intersection of 120 degrees between each intersecting line. Wherever a smaller line joins a larger one it intersects at a right angle or 90 degrees. This is the rule; however in nature there can always be found occasional exceptions.

The energy from one surface transmits to the next surface in an attempt to balance the force. This balance of energy or force creates a physical continuity between surfaces. This continuity has a very definite set of patterns, depending on the conditions.

When we look at the intersecting network of veins in a maple leaf, it first can be seen that there are almost never more than three lines coming together at one point of intersection. Where a smaller vein intersects a larger one, the angle of intersection is usually approaching, or exactly at, 90 degrees, a balance of forces for two sizes. Where three veins of equal size join, they attempt to join at an even balance also, but since they are of equal size, the angle is also equal or 120 degrees.

The same situation and the same results hold for almost all associated phenomena; the veins in the wing of a dragonfly, the arterial network in a lung,

126

or the intersections in the film membranes of soap bubbles. A cluster of bubbles between two glass plates very freely shows the results of surface energy, because there is little other force to influence them. The bubble divisions bend and contort to enable them to join at almost exactly equal angles.

In the case of cracking and splitting of drying matter, such as dehydrated mud and old cracked paint, the situation is similar but reversed. Instead of expansion, we are dealing with contraction. As the water leaches out from a once inundated field, or the oil slowly dries from a macadam street, the material

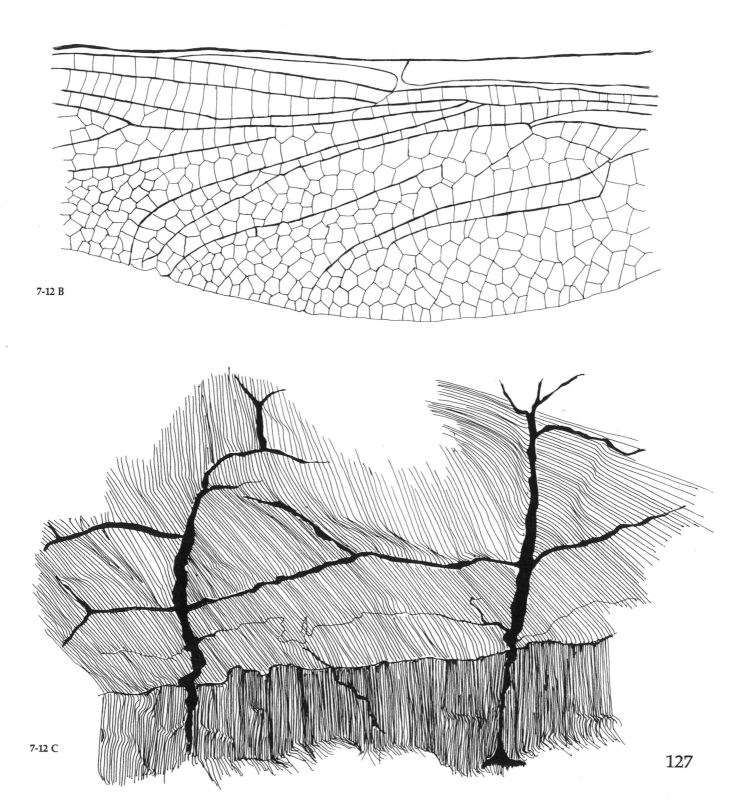

7-12 B

7-12 C

contracts, setting the whole mass into tension. When cracking begins it is usually quite rapid. Each crack will relieve a certain tension. When one crack meets another, it will most often stop, for the strains at that point have been resolved. This kind of line joining results in a three-way intersection, and the angle of intersections of equal size cracks, is on the average equal, or 120 degrees. The angles of the larger and smaller intersecting cracks come close to 90 degrees. The resulting forms are strikingly close to that found in their living counterparts.

In still other examples we might follow the reverse of nature attempting to fill a void with partitions by looking at her way of dealing with objects being packed tightly together, or how she spaces an excess of partitions. The circle, or its three dimensional equivalent, the sphere, is found throughout nature. This is because of nature's propensity for economy, for it has been pointed out that the circle or sphere gives maximum interior for minimal exterior. If a number of spherical rubber balloons were to be forcefully compressed together, their rounded surfaces would give way to a series of flat surfaces as they push against one another; their spheres would change into faceted three-dimensional forms. These forms, rhombic dodecahedron by name, have twelve equal surfaces. Each balloon would adjust itself so that it comes in contact with six balloons in its own plane; plus three balloons would press in from above and three from below. In any similar situation in any yielding material, living or non-living, the results are

the same. When seeds or cells multiply and expand, they often exactly duplicate this process, and can be seen under the microscope to be perfectly equal twelve-sided figures. Whether in the plant or animal kingdom, this situation is often duplicated.

If the balloon experiment is repeated on a two-dimensional surface using circles instead of spheres, the circles will deform into six-sided figures, or hexagons. Bubbles blown between two glass plates will form a fairly uniform hexagonal network. This hexagonal pattern is familiar to any who have observed patterns seen almost everywhere in nature.

One of the most familiar hexagonal networks is the bee's cell, or honeycomb. As the comb is under construction, each worker bee attempts to make his cell as full as possible, which compresses the cell surfaces together; the hexagonal pattern is the result. If the cells on the perimeter of the comb are examined where no others come in contact with them, they can be seen to remain rounded, for they are not subjected to close packing. One of those analogies that so delight the teleologists and those who look for a unity in the world is the simple fact that the intersecting angles of the hexagon are all at exactly 120 degrees, and all intersections are of only three members, no more and no less. This brings us right back again to our idea of space partitioning. If the parched mud plane mentioned earlier were absolutely even in its consistency and were subjected to a consistent force throughout, the cracking of its surface would produce a faultless hexagonal symmetry.

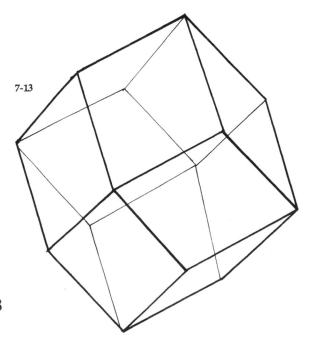

7-13

7-13 The rhombic dodecahedron with its twelve sides is formed when a sphere is compressed in a three-dimensional space.

7-14 A, B, C, D. The moth pictured above has laid a cluster of eggs on a flat surface. The eggs are spherical in form. Following laws of close packed geometry the eggs fall into a pattern that causes each to be surrounded by six others. In any similar situation the same results would occur. When circular forms are compressed together on a two-dimensional surface they contact at six points. If the circular forms are pushed together so that sides of the forms flatten, another set of laws comes into effect: the circles tend to be deformed in such a way that each juncture becomes a three-way intersection of equal angles (120 degrees) as shown with the large bubbles compressed into a small dish. If the circles are free to move about and equalize pressure they tend to become six-sided figures, or hexagons.

The bees' comb is a result of this forming process. It might be noted further that if a hexagon is divided into its component parts it will be seen that it is made up of six equilateral triangles. The equilateral triangle is essential to some very sophisticated structures of mankind (see Struts and Ties).

But the hexagon means more to us than an often-repeated pattern. The hexagonal network with its three-way joining is prominent because of its balancing and equalizing of forces. For the same reasons it is a superior structural form and hence used in some of mankind's most sophisticated structures.

There are but a few of the countless number of physical laws that weave the living and non-living into a continuous fabric, binding all together. It is hoped that this brief glance can indicate that this structural unity does exist.

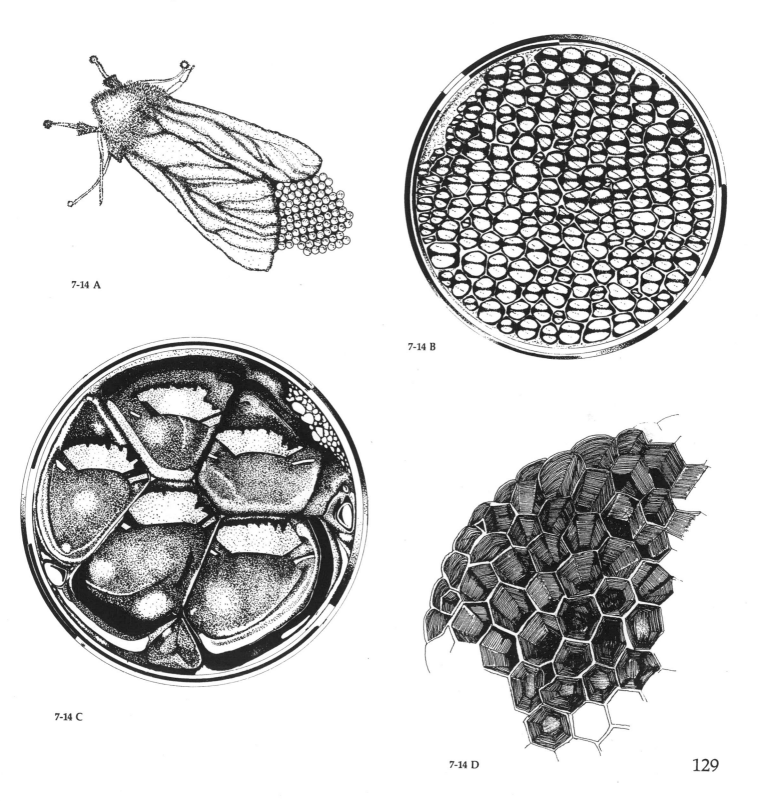

7-14 A

7-14 B

7-14 C

7-14 D

129

8 | CHANCE AND THE IRRATIONAL

It may be presumptuous to say that the form of a certain object can be analyzed logically, for in all probability more exists out of pure chance than exists by design; restrictions may come from size, structure, function and all the other physical realities of our planet. But they can do little more than suggest an outcome and leave the rest up to chance.

Chance, however, is not completely irrational, for even chance operates under a very; rigid set of laws. These laws become increasingly pervasive as the numbers increase. Nature deals with vast numbers. Each individual fish in a school of 75,000 herring will be amazingly uniform in proportion, size, and markings; in a beach of billions of grains of sand 99% of them will vary only fractionally from the mean weight.

If a choice is to be determined by chance with a two-way, yes-no, binary solution and both are exactly equal, systematic prediction of outcome is impossible. Prediction of outcome in events of small numbers is hardly better, but predictability of chance outcome in large numbers is not only possible, it is an iron-bound law. The greater the number of chances, the more accurately the gross outcome can be predicted, and still each individual chance is not influenced by those that come before and those that come after. Each occurrence within the larger number of occurrences is independent, for in the laws of chance the past *cannot* affect the future.

Experienced gamblers know the laws of averages well, but still keep notation cards as events unfold at the tables with the belief that the time might come to move one way or another. For in spite of rationality, they believe that somehow that past events must influence the overall ratios to sway the future. The idea of "runs," something happening over a series of times, is prevalent.

When an event like the spinning of a coin with a heads or tails choice occurs ten times there may be six heads to four tails, or a difference of twenty percent. In 1000 tries maybe 520 to 480 will appear, or a difference of 40 in 1000. In a certain experiment an accurately balanced coin was spun 100,000 times and the results were not astonishing to those who are familiar with the laws of large numbers: 50,039 to 49,961 or a difference of 78 in 100,000 or just 39 above the perfect 50/50 ratio. But it is still necessary to be reminded that each spinning of the coin is independent of those that precede and follow.

It has been said that odds of one to one thousand million is the same as impossible, and rationally that seems to be true, but in pure chance nothing *but* the improbable can happen.

Let us say that a roulette wheel with its 36 numbers is spun four times. A series of four numbers must appear. Any combination has equal chance, perhaps 21-17-3-11 appears or 19-16-33-30. These random

8-1 With the spinning of a coin and other two-way decisions averages are easy to determine, but with multiplying decisions the situation becomes more complex. Let us use, for an example an arrangement of little roof-shaped forms, the peak of each arising under the eaves of the two just above. If all are perfectly centered and a great quantity of balls were to fall through the maze landing exactly on the peak of the roof, each drop would yield a 50/50 chance of falling to the left or right side of the roof. The numbers indicate the percentages of the total numbers of balls to pass that point.

The figures are the amounts that the balls "should" take given the law of averages. If a dozen balls were to be passed through the maze it is unlikely that anything near these averages would appear; a thousand would be close and ten thousand would be almost perfect.

At the bottom of the maze the balls fall to the ground and form a pile in the shape of a bell curve, fewer and fewer departing more and more from the center. D'Arcy Thompson had said of the bell curve, "It rises to a maximum, falls away on either side, has neither beginning or end. It is normally symmetrical, for lack of cause to make it otherwise, it falls off faster and then slower the further it departs from the mean or middle line… It changes its curvature and from being concave to the middle line spreads out to become convex."

The bell curve has many analogies in the laws of chance. By way of example, let us say that this curve represents not a pile of balls but the variation from a mean weight in the manufacture of a simple industrial commodity like nails. Nails are sold by the pound, and manufacturers expect them to all be within a very narrow range of weight per nail. However, there will always be a slight deviation above and below that perfect weight. If a large number of nails of a certain type and size were to be individually weighed, it would be found that the deviation above and below that mean weight, shown graphically, would be a bell curve.

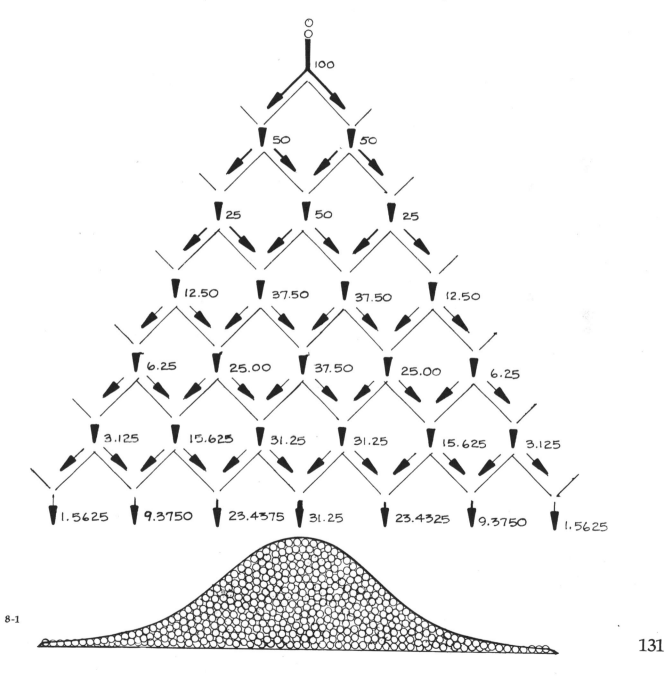

8-1

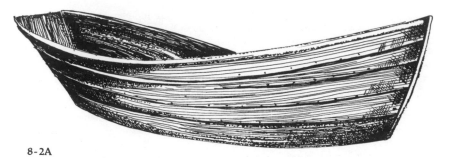

8-2A

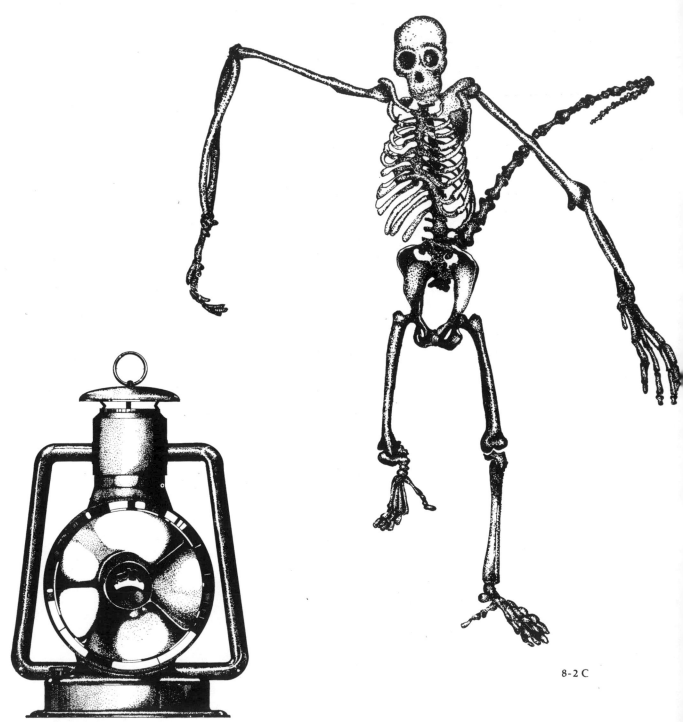

8-2 C

8-2 B

numbers are unnoticeable, but should a 1-2-3-4 series or a 1-1-1-1, or 36-36-36-36 appear, the viewer would be astounded; yet these number would have equal chances of coming up with any other series of numbers. The chances of any certain combination of four is one to 1,679,615. A million and a half to one, you might believe, is a near impossibility, which is to say, that any one *particular* combination is also nearly impossible.

If a design is very carefully conceived and all criteria taken into account, and then executed with utmost fidelity, how can chance stand in the face of this rationality? What effect does chance play on the designs of people?

Let us say a ship's hull was to be designed as responsively as possible to the requirements of its use. The designer would take into account displacement, speed, propulsion, depth, width, length, steering, horsepower, water salinity, water temperature, wave condition, wind condition, air resistance, material of hull, paint surface, marine organisms, corrosion, and thousands of other factors. These conditions and requirements might be given to the powers of computer logic, with instructions to produce a set of lateral and longitudinal cross-sections of the hull. The curving sections would approximate the hull in a skeletal form.

But despite the sincere attempts of human and electronic brains, little can be done but suggest an adequate solution.

Each lateral cross-section of the hull is composed of compounded curves, roughly a "U" shape; the cross-sections change as they move through the length of the ship. The longitudinal lines represent a bird's-eye view of sections from top deck to keel.

8-2 A, B, C. The fishing dory, kerosene lantern, and the monkey are examples of forms that have reached a high level of sophistication. Two have stopped development: the dory and the lantern, whereas the monkey continues on the path of survival with modification, refinement, and gradual improvement as its species continues. The 1900 kerosene lantern is the culmination of thousands of years of technological improvements in wick burning lanterns. It is a form well on its way to its adoptive peak (see text). The development of the technology of wick burning lamps has all but stopped because the need has shifted with the introduction of electric lighting. It is conceivable that again as economics change the kerosene wick lantern will again be in demand and it will continue in its progress to its adoptive peak.

The dory has been in use by fishermen for many years. Its form has evolved, improved, and endured up to the present. Those who know it well think that it is truly a superior craft for its use and the conditions that it must encounter. Now its development has stopped because the methods of fishing no longer place it in demand.

From the point of view of hydrodynamics, the form of the hull of a ship should be a perfect diagram of the water moving past it with the least possible drag causing turbulence. If the conditions through which the ship passed were static, if all the variables of wind and wave were constant, it would still be next to impossible to find the perfect hull configuration, for the choices are infinite. There are an infinite number of variations of a single curve; even within a narrow range of change each cross-section can be varied infinitely. We have no ability to say what the best solution is. Added to this is the fact that the conditions change from moment to moment, as the environment through which the ship passes is shifting constantly. Beyond this there is even dispute as to the general approach to designing the best hull form for maximum efficiency. It might be that a flexible skin is the best. Furthermore, to be a responsive design, other considerations must be accounted for which will further influence the final form; factors such as cost of manufacture and operation, load carrying and distribution, cargo transfer, docking or mooring, and the many human factors. The final results, as with the cargo ships that are now in service, are hardly more than impotent attempts formed as much by chance and default as by design. (44)

Chance is just as responsible for things existing as not existing. Heredity and function determine the general direction of form; material and structure modify results. Size, physical law, and the ecophenotypic effect further control the outcome; but chance, the irrational factor, must always balance the determinable.

An evolving form may be adapting to a specific functional problem, but a problem which has several solutions even under these existing constraints. One of these solutions may evolve rather than another, not as a result of a selection process but by simple chance. Theoretical biologists have constructed a topographical model to illustrate the path of chance through a landscape of possible developments. The evolving lineage begins in a low basin. About it the terrain mounts through hills, corridors and mountains to adoptive peaks. Some of the peaks are considerably higher than others, meaning that they are closer to the optimal solution. The developing lineage can only climb an inclining slope if it is improving through natural selection.

To descend after attaining a certain level means to become less successful, which is contrary to nature's and man's selection process. But if that lineage is 133 developing up a slope that takes it to a lesser adoptive peak, at the top of the peak the lineage must cease to develop, though it is far from optimal. For the lineage to reach the top of an adjoining higher adoptive peak it would have to descend the mountainside beneath it to the valley and climb to the higher peak, or move backwards to begin again. The only release from this situation is if the landscape itself were to change, the mountain to crumble beneath. In nature this would be a major environmental change, like a coming ice age. With the man-made it would be less calamitous and could result from the shifting of usage and the expiration of a need.

We tend to think of all that is in nature as exemplifying the best solutions and think that anything that does not exist is impossible. This is not necessarily true. At some point back in the recesses of animal development movement by legs, pedal locomotion, possibly through chance, moved from the valleys to the mountains — taking all the walking species up the terrain leading to adoptive peaks. None of the species that move over the ground on legs may have yet reached the optimum, but there as a group we stand still or climb higher. Possibly only a new kingdom could adopt an entirely new form of movement. It has been pointed out that with no more complexity than the development of a lobster claw, a coasting wheel could have evolved to move creatures over the ground. The coasting wheel, like those on a cart or the front wheel on a bicycle, is relatively simple to construct in nature. But a powered wheel, the back wheel on a bicycle, might not be possible with natural means. It is possible that the coasting wheel represents an adoptive peak that has been preempted by the peak of pedal locomotion. (45)

Another example may be found in the lack of organisms using sails and wind power to travel over the surface of the water. Though this does occur in a very primitive form of jellyfish, it is surprising that a fully developed and sophisticated system, with full maneuverability, has not evolved, unless the role of chance has been significant.

There are many examples of man's devices reaching adoptive peaks that are far from optimal. We have been saddled with the use of the gasoline internal combustion engine in transportation and industry, though it is obviously far from optimal and seems to have moved very close to its adoptive peak. The change will probably come about by the adoptive peak disappearing beneath as usage and demand diminish.

One hundred odd elements, placed in tens of thousands of combinations, under hundreds of thousands of natural and human societal forces, within billions of types of environmental conditions, produce an infinity of forms. The incredible fact is not that there are so many possibilities of form, but that they are derived from such a small base of matter.

To catalog the elements and their combinations is a simple task when contemplating the immensity of forces that mold them. We have listed but a few of the major ones in this book. The reader should not assume that this is more than an indication, for systems and magnitudes of forces blossom into infinities upon infinities. Perhaps we should marvel not at the variety of form but at the interconnections that make it possible to even consider some definitions as the earth's materials are compressed and flattened, twisted and perforated, stretched and eroded, cracked and smoothed.

Man's inheritance from nature and his accumulation of influence and invention throughout history is far more flexible than that which is found in the natural world. There are many untouched adoptive peaks that must be explored. We must take care not to change the good for the bad, and the efficient for the inefficient. A clarity of thought and a comprehending overview are necessary to re-evaluate the less than optimal solutions and create new and better ones.

8-3 Any form evolving to a better solution, a more adoptive design, follows a path that only rises. The evolving form begins developing at some low point, the path takes it constantly to higher ground, en route there are many branching divisions that lead to other hills or mountains; some may be high; still others may have towering possibilities. The choice at many branches is determined only by chance. Once the design is upon the slope, to turn around is impossible because the adoptive process must lead only to a "better" solution, or higher up. When the peak is surmounted development must stop, for the design has reached its maximum form. Other forms may be abandoned on the path for the adoptive process has ceased through disuse.

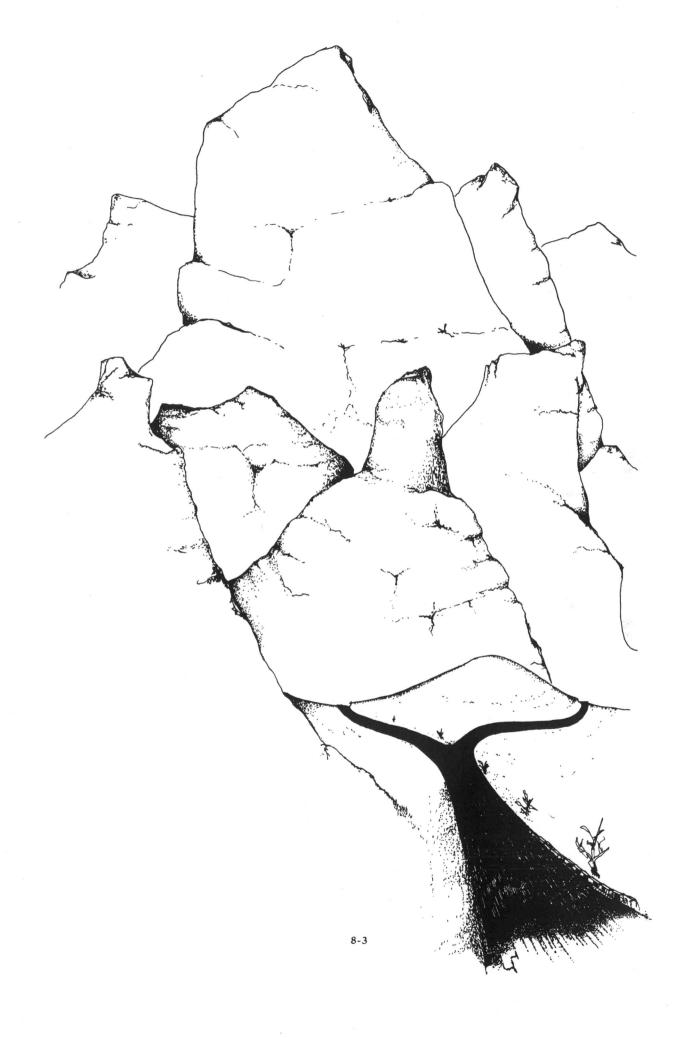

8-3

NOTES

*The numbers listed to the left of the notes indicate the page or pages of the text where the corresponding source material is used or quoted.

Numbers in parenthesis refer to the paragraphs on the page.

1 FORM AND MATTER

12 (1) There are two basic classes into which substances can be divided, elements and compounds. Elements are materials in their simplest form. They differ from one another in such things as boiling point, melting point, density, hardness, ductility and compressibility. Elements cannot be decomposed or further simplifed by ordinary chemical means. Iron, aluminum and calcium are among the basic elements. Compounds are comprised of two or more elements united in definite proportions by weight. When combining elements to form a compound a chemical reaction must take place. Salt is an example of a compound, for it is made from the elements sodium and chlorine. A mixture differs from a compound in that it is a random jumble of two or more elements or compounds in no particular proportion and with no particular chemical structure. No chemical reaction is necessary to bring mixtures into or out of existence.

Kenneth Oakley in Charles Singer, E.J. Holmyard and A.R. Hall, A History of Technology, Vol I (London: Oxford University Press, 1956), pp. 10-11.

14 (2) It might seem to be stating the obvious to define just what gasses, liquids and solids are; however, there are some materials that appear to be what they are not and others that, in some conditions, seem to lie between two states. Glass, for example, so gradually moves from a liquid state into a solid state that it is impossible to say at any point which it is. The following are some basic guides for definition:

Solids — have a definite shape and volume, they resist a compressive force, a tensional force, and a shearing force (for a definition of these terms please see Chapter 2). Solids will, though, yield to all three over time and/or with the exertion of enough force. Solids resemble liquids in that they both have a definite volume. But solids do not need a lateral support to maintain their shape; in other words, they do not need a container. Solids differ from both liquids and gasses in that they have a definite shape.

Liquids — resemble solids in that they have volume, but will flow into the shape of the containing vessel in a limited amount of time and with little force. Liquids at slow speeds will not resist shear; the higher the viscosity, or the less the tendency to flow, and the greater the velocity of the force the greater the resistance to shear. Liquids contained in a vessel resist compression but do not resist tension.

Gasses — have neither a definite volume nor shape; they will flow into and fill any form and any sized vessel, they are infinitely expandable, they get less and less dense as they expand. All gasses condense into liquids or solids when sufficiently cooled and compressed. When the temperature increases the volume increases. Gasses resist compression if contained, but not tension. They do not resist shear at slow velocity, but show increasing resistance when exposed to a shearing force at increasing high veiocity. Both liquids and gasses are defined as fluids.

17 (3) The lesson of geology is universal. All energies and substances move to the compromise, high to the low, numerous to the sparse, live to the dead, moist to the dry, and heat to the lack of heat. This is the law of the evolution and the world, the principle of entropy. When all these energies and potential energies are spent, or being spent, entropy is increased. A net increase of entropy is the predestination of an aging universe. Entropy is the equalizing process by which the universe is moving through a state of chaos and disorder to an end in which all is of one temperature, energy and work cease to exist, everything is inert and uniform and the universe is dead.

In terms of simple definition entropy is the measure of the capacity of a system to undergo a spontaneous change of heat. The study of heat, thermodynamics, is directly linked to the whole aging process of the universe. Thermodynamics is probably the most basic branch of science for it deals with matter, energy, and time. It is based upon three laws:

1. Heat can be converted into work and work into heat. The amount of work is always equal to the quantity of heat. Heat can be expressed in energy. *2.* When a free exchange of heat takes place between two bodies as a self-sustaining and continuous process, the heat must always be transferred from the hotter to the colder body. *3.* Every substance has a definite entropy (availability of energy to do work) that approaches zero as its temperature approaches absolute zero.

It is possible to move in space in a backwards or forwards direction but only one direction of travel is possible in time because of the Second Law of Thermodynamics. The heat must always move from the hotter to the colder; the reverse is not possible. If a ball is dropped from a window, when it strikes the ground a small amount of heat is dissipated into the air from this action. If time were to reverse the ball would bounce back to its point of impact, re-absorb the heat given off during impact and it would fly up to the window where it began its trip. By the Second Law the heat cannot be re-absorbed and the action cannot be reversed and so time and the universe move on in only one direction.

18 (4) It should be noted that there are some kinds of matter that are without an organized structure and to all extent formless. When minerals are without a crystalline structure they are said to be amorphous. These can be solids like clay, limestone, or glass. Crystalline material can be mechanically or chemically broken down so that the crystals no longer exist, and so be made into an amorphous solid. If a substance is made up of non-crystalline particles that are larger than molecules, usually in a liquid, semi-liquid, or gaseous state, it is called a colloid. Milk, mayonnaise and smoke are all colloids. Organic tissue is often found to be in a colloidal mass, but the mass is usually contained by a more structured cell wall.

22 (5) Friction is defined as the resistance offered to the sliding or rolling of one surface over another. In man's uses it can be both necessary and burdensome. Without friction, car tires would not move the car forward nor stop it, the driver's hands would not be able to control the steering wheel and the driver of the automobile would have a hard time staying in place on the seat. However, the car engine would scarcely ever wear out without friction. The surface quality and the pressure are the two most important factors controlling friction. When the pressure is excessive and/or the surface is rough there is a great deal of friction and heat is produced with movement.

22 (6) A consideration of the intersection of different kinds of materials and how they mutually affect each other is necessary. Gaskets are used between mating parts of machinery to compromise the slight imperfections in the surface and enable them to join solidly. Coatings, paint, case hardening, and plating all help to better suit the material to its

environment of use. Some materials oxidize and so control their own surface changes, and actually grow more resistant to wear and chemical action as they are used; the oxidation helps reduce further oxidation.

22 (7) Depending upon the type of material and the type of wearing action, the substance that is removed from these worn surfaces is sometimes re-deposited in the low irregularities. This smoothes the whole surface, effecting a polishing or glazing. Sometimes the removed material will chafe over the surface without anchoring to one place; the effect of this can further speed the wearing away of the surface.

23 (8) Commonly lubricants are in a liquid state; the very thin ones penetrate the surfaces to a greater degree and offer a lubricating surface as thin as one molecule. Thin lubricants are useful for high speed movements; the greases are used for slow moving parts, heavy loads and reciprocating journals. The former is called thin film lubrication and the latter is fluid film lubrication. Both replace the dry friction condition. The "slipperiness" of oils and greases comes from their molecular composition and their viscosity or resistance to flow away. On the opposite end of that scale would be such fluids as alcohol and ether with almost no lubricating qualities. The "slipperiness" of the dry lubricants such as graphite and talc comes from the shapes of the particles of which they are made.

2 STRUTS AND TIES

36 (9) There are several kinds of conditions of loading that engineers must take into account when building. Primarily, there is the constant weight of the structure itself. This is called the *dead load; live load* is the term applied to transitory moveable objects that are supported by the structure, like vehicles crossing a bridge or people and furniture in a building. *Impact* and *resonate loads* fall under the general term *dynamic loading;* often arising when certain unusual conditions occur. Large buildings must structure against *wind loading.*

36 (10) It is interesting to note the path of weight transfer from the bicycle rider to the ground. Since the bicycle spokes are tensional they cannot support the weight from below, but must hang it. The rider's weight is transferred through the frame to the wheel axel. It is then suspended by several of the topmost spokes on the wheel, and transferred to the rim and to the ground.

36 (11) Bending and buckling can be expected in a bar supporting weight in compression but not a bar holding weight in tension. But bending in pure compression is, in theory, avoidable. If the supporting materials were of absolutely pure consistency so that the strength were equal throughout, if the piece were finished with perfect dimensions, if the load and resistance were completely uniform and all other factors were equal and even, only in such a case would there be no failure through bending, no matter how long and how thin the piece was. However, failure would occur when the piece in compression was actually pressed shorter. A situation of absolute uniformity is, of course, impossible. In most standard conditions, bending and buckling are avoided only by increased lateral dimensions, thus adding weight. This problem can be avoided by the use of tension rather than compression.

42 (12) All animals with internal skeletons have the same vocabulary of bones—reworked to fit their needs. The bat for instance has essentially all the corresponding bones the human has, but in totally different proportions. The pelvis on the bat is about the same size as its elbow joint, the bones of the leg are much smaller than the bones of the arm, and the longest group of bones are those that make up what corresponds to the index finger.

49 (13) Buckminster Fuller has pointed to the definition of these three basic structures, "There are only three possible cases of Fundamental Omnisymmetrical, Omnitriangulated least

effort structural systems in nature; the tetrahedron with three triangles at each vertex, the octahedron with four triangles at each vertex, and the icosahedron with five triangles at each vertex. If there are six equilateral triangles around a vertex we cannot define a three dimensional structural system, only a plane." Fuller goes on to explain the spatial qualities of these three fundamental forms, "Of the three fundamental structures the tetrahedron contains the most surface and the most structural quanta per volume, it is therefore the strongest structure per unit of volume. On the other hand, the icosahedron provides the most volume with the least surface and least structural quanta per unit of volume and, though least strong, it is structurally stable and gives therefore the most efficient volume per unit of invested structural quanta."

Quote from R. Buckminster Fuller, Synergetics *(New York: Macmillan, 1975).*

49 (14) The sphere is nature's most spacious form, an absolute maximum enclosed volume with a minimum enclosing surface. There is no other form that can accomplish this as well. The dome, which is made from the hemisphere and its many variations, offers some of the qualities of the sphere, and is an excellent form for man's shelter needs. The dome, however, is better suited to large scale than small. At small size the interior space is poorly used because of the inclined walls. Application of building materials is difficult in a small dome, for they don't readily conform to a greatly curved surface and angles other than ninety degrees. At large sizes these problems are not present.

51 (15) There are two categories of structures: freestanding, independent structures that are self-contained like a bicycle wheel or a sailboat, and dependent structures that rely upon their environment to hold them intact, like suspension bridges or spiderwebs.

51 (16) There is evidence some Greek architects used the arch but its significance was not recognized by the vast majority of Greek builders.

3 SIZE

54 (17) *Quote from D'Arcy Thompson,* On Growth and Form, *Vol. I (Cambridge: Cambridge University Press, 1959), p. 51.*

60 (18) The stomach of a human is comprised of millions of cells, the stomach of a mouse has fewer; the primitive digestive system of the microscopic rotifers must operate with a relatively small number of cells to perform essentially the same task. The phenomenon of the relationship of cell size to organ size is even more pronounced in the case of the rod and cone cells of animal eyes. The size of animal eyes does not vary in proportion to the size of their bodies; small creatures have proportionately larger eyes than the large creatures. This is because the eye responds primarily to the wave-length of light; considering only optics, large eyes are no better than small eyes. The same amount of visual information can be gathered by a marble-sized eye as by a softball-sized eye.

63 (19) The African baobab tree grows of soft, pithy wood to enormous dimensions. The larger of these trees have great bulbous trunks and very thick limbs. The wide girth of the limb in this soft wood is needed to structure the tree against gravity. In a descending range of scale, the forms of the living correspond less to the effects of gravity. The larger mammals are structured with a massive framework which the exterior of their body reflects; there is no sharp division between torso and limb. An internal skeletal structure would be impractical to the insect, so the shell takes over the job of giving structure to the body of the insect. With a hard shell the body of the insect tends to be more a unit or series of units; there is a definite separation between abdomen and legs. As the scale grows smaller the animal forms tend to be more spherical. The microscopic animals are mostly simple

137

spherical or ovoid forms. There can be found exceptions to the above, but the general tendency holds true.

68 (20) The principles involved in the metabolism and habits of animals in relation to their size and conservation of heat are set forth in Bergman's Law.

Quote from D'Arcy Thompson, On Growth and Form, (Cambridge: Cambridge University Press, 1959), Vol I, p. 34.

4 THE FORMS OF FUNCTION

73 (21) The term "form follows function" was first spoken by the artist and critic Horatio Greenough and later promoted by architects Louis Sullivan and Frank Lloyd Wright. It rose out of the reaction against the powerful influences of the picturesque and decorative in the arts, especially architecture. The term has been championed by the "Functionalists" ever since.

74 (22) Whether we speak of natural or man made design, in terms of functionalism, our reference is to a working or utilitarian design. But as David Pye has pointed out, a steel pylon carrying electric wires does not carry them any better than a marble column would, yet we call the marble column decorative and the steel pylon utilitarian. What then is the difference? The answer seems that one is more economic to build and erect, so perhaps economy then is one of the most important concepts of design.

77 (23) *Quote from R.A. Salsman in Charles Singer, E.J. Holmyard, and A.R. Hall, A History of Technology, Vol. III (London: Oxford University Press, 1956) pp. 116-117.*

79 (24) There are many examples of the multi-purpose in nature. Animals use teeth, horns, claws, trunks, for eating, fighting, courting, digging, lifting, climbing and all kinds of actions other than the more obvious "purpose" of the appendage. The concept of make-do is very common in nature. Conversely, the specialized is also common. There can be found bird's bills that have elongated greatly, and anteaters with sticky tongues to satisfy highly specialized feeding habits.

80 (25) *Quote from David Pye, The Nature of Design, (New York: Reinhold Publishing Corporation, 1964).*

81 (26) There is a tendency for man to begin with a design of simple clarity and then move gradually into an obscurity of form, where the function becomes lost in embellishment not always necessary to the function, and sometimes at odds with it. The Greek Doric order was a clear direct statement that almost became lost in the decorative influences of the Ionic, and still later the Corinthian orders. The first automobiles contained a clarity of form and function since lost in their coverings. However, if one were never to have seen a lobster claw or an Eskimo kayak in action, by the very form of its visually articulated design, its purpose and the service that it renders would be come obvious.

83 (27) A salmon swimming upstream has been shown to be the most efficient moving thing known, in terms of calorie consumption, time required and distance travelled. Second only to the salmon is a person on a bicycle. Near the bottom of this list are cars, cows, rodents, and walking people.

A list of a few more elegant designs might include the following: McCormick reaper, cotton gin, kayak, bow and arrow, suspension bridge, climbing equipment, pick axe, kite, glider, racing scull, sickle, scissor, Stilson wrench, Flexible Flyer sled, one horse sleigh, umbrella, spoon, ball point pen. You probably can think of other worthwhile candidates. Probably the extreme expression of design elegance is the self-regulating system, a functioning system that controls itself by its own devices automatically. Most animals have heat controls that automatically regulate body temperature by controlling disposition of the blood and the sweat glands. The thermostat coupled with the heating furnace is a self-regulating device (sometimes called feedback control). A self-regulating design of simple elegance can be

found in the mountain communities of Southwestern Romania. In this region, the winter is cold and damp, the summer dry and hot. The people cover their houses with shingles notched with grooves to fit into one another. The shingles are made from a wood that is very reactive to moisture change, expanding when wet and contracting when dry. In the winter the shingles are expanded tightly on each other, locking out the weather. In the summer they dry and contract and allow the breeze to move through the house.

85 (28) *Quote from David Bohm in C.H. Waddington, Towards a Theoretical Biology, Vol. II (Edinburgh: Edinburgh University Press, 1969) p. 43.*

5 THE GENERATIONS

86 (29) Intelligence is our way of coping with the situations of our environment. But it is not the only way to survive. Many highly successful societies in the animal kingdom operate through the use of elaborate and sophisticated instinct refined through millions of generations and passed down genetically as a gift of birth, with no need to accumulate knowledge individual by individual as we must.

88 (30) Most of the products of the early technologies helped to better the human condition. Not the least part of this goal was the lessening of physical labor. Human muscle power was technology's first major power source, called the prime mover; next came domesticated animals, to act on human directions. Tools and machines were innovated to transform animal energy into work. Moving air and falling water were the first non-living prime movers (windmills and water wheels) to be used on a large scale. As the prime movers became more sophisticated the machine was integrated with them. For several hundred years wood- and later coal-fired steam was the prime mover. Oil then gasoline took over at the turn of the 19th century. At this writing, it is uncertain what will be next — possibly many alternatives. The action has shifted from the human working with his hands and hand tools to the machine creating its own force and directing its own actions.

93 (31) Incredibly, there are today still a few human societies that have escaped any diffusion of technology. They are scattered about the globe excluded from the accumulated knowledge of the rest of mankind. These societies number perhaps a total of fewer individuals than the population of a small town, but their micro-evolution is important, for each represents the remnants of a complete culture, tradition, language, and history of artifacts of a linear society. The Tasaday Indians are such a society—a stone age culture surviving by the existence of only about twenty-five people hidden among the mountains and forest canopy of New Guinea in the time of Bio-electronics and artificial intelligence.

99 (32) All these residual effects of the passing generations of technology are not negative. One among others is sometimes useful; the delay action between invention and integration of new technology is often a positive thing, for it acts like a mechanical damper. This inhibits too free and quick a response, thus preventing the oscillation of an uncontrolled back-and-forth movement or energy level from one extreme to the other. The influence of past generations that persists into the present tends to act as a damper, bridging false starts, temporary and provincial solutions, and so allows only the significant and universal contributions to seep into the stream of technology.

One half of all the world's inventions have occured since 1965. With this rapidity, inventions enter the mainstream more readily, thus allowing greater deviation of quality and more short-lived technology.

Quote from Siegfried Giedion, Mechanization Takes Command (New York: Oxford University Press, 1948), p. 152.

6 THE ECOPHENOTYPIC EFFECT

102 (33) Eco-, from ecological, phenotype (as in phenomenon, observable occurrence), the observable appearance of an organism. An organism also consists of a genotype, the genetic constitution, as distinguished from its physical appearance. Phylogeny (Phylogenesis) is the evolutionary development of a Phylum (of any plant or animal). Ontogeny is the course of development of an individual organism.

105 (34) *Quote from Siegfried Giedion*, Mechanization Takes Command *(New York: Oxford University Press, 1948), p. 46.*

107 (35) A very original American by the name of Oliver Evans was one of the first to contrive a fully automated production system. The product was milled grain, the date was 1785. Evans seized five known inventions, marshalled them into a system and let his milling crew go home. Evan's mill, as most American mills, operated on water, the wheel giving power only to the stone. But there was a power surplus, ample enough to be shunted to do all the other tasks involved in milling. Hitherto a man carried the grain in sacks from the farmer's wagon to the top of the mill. Evans replaced this operation with a conveyer and buckets. The farmer merely shoveled his whole grain into these buckets. Evans replaced the hopper boy with a mechanical rake to aerate and guide the grain to the chutes; a second conveyer moved the grain horizontally; an Archimedes' screw moved the grain to the stone; and finally a delivery system returned the ground grain to the farmer. The complete operation required no human power or guidance and was activated by one water wheel.

108 (36) Fifteen parts manufactured by fifteen people is not an extreme example of specialization and Division of Labor. It is possible that there could be a dozen people involved in the manufacture of each part.

109 (37) In line flow production a moving conveyer delivers the assembly of parts to the assembly station. There a person makes the addition by hand. The assembly process is still largely under the domination of the human, for assembly often requires complex maneuvers. The machine is not incapable of these maneuvers, but the simple fact is that often the human assembler comes cheaper than the complex machine. It is almost inevitable that machines will take over all these tasks eventually.

It is not the purpose of this book to make judgements on the rewards or misery of work. We have come through the injustices of slave labor and the horrors of toiling in a mine shaft in seventeenth century Europe. Today the factory worker survives but is merely bored. But is just surviving enough? David Bohm has said, "Any society which puts mere survival as the supreme value of life is already on the way to collective decay. — Functions make sense only when the ultimate aim of this function is beauty, harmony, and a creative life for all."

110 (38) *This quotation is paraphased from D'Arcy Thompson.*

111 (39) Today inventors and designers originate new artifacts and improve and change old ones. They look upon their task as requiring that they deliver finished products to the market, thus excluding the consumer from any of the creative process. Let us imagine if the designers were to design not an automobile, but a superb motor, or transmission, or a chassis, an auto body, or fenders, or even a system of assembly. Let us say further that these components, or combinations of components, were interchangeable, made to be used in unlimited assemblies. The automobile buyer would study the catalogues, and select just the combination of size, type and power of engine, transmission, seats, headlights, etc. that is desired. Monopolies would be challenged, and decentralization of production would be encouraged, thus allowing thousands of small producers to compete on the open market, and the possibility of local manufacture would occur. Highly individualized products would be common.

The key to this system would be unlimited variation with standardization of fit and tolerance allowing interchangeability. The consumer would creatively participate in the whole process. The buyer would have the option of some, all, or none of the assembly. A number of local assemblies would emerge for various products.

This system would bring us back to complete the full circle; the individual would again have creative option and become a generalist. Instead of working raw materials into artifacts however, he would work manufactured components into new products.

7 TELEOLOGY

114 (40) *Quote from D'Arcy Thompson*, On Growth and Terms, Vol. 1 *(Cambridge: Cambridge University Press, 1959) p. 13.*

117 (41) The growth pattern of a complex organism like the human is remarkable to imagine. It is amazing that the appearance of a person remains as static as it does when one considers all that goes on to maintain a relatively unchanging form. Every part of the body is consistently being replaced, and with the immature expansion also takes place. The torso, limbs, fingers, toes, hair, fingernails, ears, etc. all grow at different rates. Within the lungs, intestine, liver, pores, cells all have different commands and needs and life spans. All this specialization must be organized into a harmony, like a phalanx of several billion soldiers remaining in line and step over plane, forest and mountain.

120 (42) Theoretical biologists, mathematicians, physical engineers and chemists have begun to find a common ground when comparing pattern, rhythm, and form (both animate and inanimate). It has been shown that the surfaces of certain regular forms, spheres, cubes, etc., deform in predictable surface patterns when subjected to sound waves, vibration or other oscillation. Conversely, countless experiments have been attempted with liquids or dry powder on metal sheets that are subject to controlled oscillation. Vibration causes the powder to form into patterns. The forms produced called CHLADNI figures, are not only often predictable but exhibit regular patterns and often are reminiscent of biological forms.

It is beyond the scope of this book to say how and why they produce these forms; however, theoretical scientists increasingly reinforce the thesis that the similarities go beyond coincidence. See *Cymatics* in the Bibliography.

125 (43) *Quote from Heinrich Hertel*, Machine, Form and Movement *(New York: Reinhold Publishing Corporation, 1966), p. 124.*

8 CHANCE AND THE IRRATIONAL

133 (44) It has been found that the porpoise moving through the water with its pliable skin does so with ease because the skin actually reshapes itself to the dynamics of the moving water, and so reduces pockets of drag.

Hull design has been improved with the relatively new notion of placing a large spherical projection ahead of the bow on tankers below the waterline, thus preventing a situation of drag just behind the bow.

134 (45) The only known true rotory motion in nature has been found in the microscopic paranema. Until recently it was thought that the flagellum, a tail-like appendage, was moving back and forth, but new data revealed that it actually rotates in a continuous motion from a socket within the body of the animal. At this writing the mechanism for this rotary motion is not known.

BIBLIOGRAPHY

1 FORM AND MATTER

Bierlein, John C. "The Journal Bearing," *Scientific American*, (July 1975) Vol. 233, No. 1, p. 50.

Cameron, A. *Basic Lubrication Theory*. London: Longman Press, 1971.

Gamow, George. *One, Two, Three, Infinity, Facts and Speculations of Science*. New York: The New American Library, 1947.

Hansen, Jans Jurgen (ed.). *Architecture in Wood*, trans. Janet Seligman. New York: Viking Press, 1971.

Hitchcock, H. *In the Nature of Materials*. New York: Sloan, 1942.

Hoffman, Branesh. *The Strange Story of the Quantum*. New York: Dover Publications, Inc., 1958.

Hsiung Li, Wen, and Lai Lam Sau. *Principles of Fluid Mechanics*. Reading, Massachusetts: Addison-Wesley Publishing Co., Inc., 1964.

Landon, J.W. *Examples in the Theory of Structure.* London: Cambridge University Press, 1932.

Wulff, John (ed.). *The Structure and Properties of Materials* (4 Vols.). New York: John Wiley and Sons, Inc., 1966.

2 STRUTS AND TIES

Beresford, Evans J. *Form in Engineering Design*. London: Oxford, The Clarendon Press, 1954.

Goss, Charles Mayo (ed.) *Gray's Anatomy*. Philadelphia: Lea and Febiger, 1959.

Gray, J. "Studies in Animal Locomotion, The Propulsive Powers of the Dolphin", *The Journal of Experimental Biology*. Vol. 13, No. 2 (1936), pp. 192-199.

Griffin, Donald R. et. al. *Readings from Scientific American, Animal Engineering*. San Francisco: W.H. Freeman and Co., 1974.

Hammond, Rolt. *The Forth Bridge and Its Builders*. Covent Gardens, England: Eyre and Spottiswoode Ltd., 1964.

Lawrence, J. Fogel. *Biotechnology: Concepts and Applications*. Englewood Cliffs, Prentice Hall, 1963.

Museum of Modern Art, The. *The Architecture of Bridges*. New York: The Museum of Modern Art, 1949.

Nervi, Pier Luigi. *Structures and Designs*, trans. Giuseppina and Mario Salvadori. New York: McGraw-Hill, 1956.

Roland, Conrad. *Frei Otto: Structures*. London: Longman Press, 1970.

Salvadori, M. and R. Heller. *Structure in Architecture*. New Jersey: Englewood Cliffs: Prentice Hall, Inc., 1965.

Seigel, Curt. *Structure and Form in Modern Architecture*. New York: Reinhold Publishing Corporation, 1962.

Torroja, E. *Philosophy of Structures*. Berkeley: University of California Press, 1958.

Whitney, Charles S. *Bridges, a Study of Their Art, Science and Evolution*. New York: Rudge, 1929.

3 SIZE

Bland, John. *Forests of Lilliput: The Realm of Mosses and Lichens*. New Jersey, Englewood Cliffs: Prentice Hall, 1971.

Conel, J. LeRoy. *Life as Revealed by the Microscope, an Interpretation of Evolution*. New York: Philosophical Library, 1969

Curtis, Helena. *The Marvelous Animals*. Garden City, New York: Natural History Press, 1968.

Gluck, Irvin. *Optics*. New York: Holt, Rinehart and Winston, Inc., 1964.

Soleri, Paolo. *Sketchbook of Paolo Soleri*. Cambridge, Mass.: M.I.T. Press, 1971.

4 THE FORMS OF FUNCTION

Doblin, Jay. *One Hundred Great Product Designs*. New York: Van Nostrand Reinhold Co., 1970.

Greenough, Horatio. *Form and Function*. Berkeley, California: University of California Press, 1957.

Pye, David. *The Nature of Design*. New York: Reinhold Publishing Corporation, 1964.

Rand, Paul. *Thoughts on Design*. New York: Van Nostrand Reinhold Co., 1970.

Royce, Joseph. *Surface Anatomy*. Philadelphia: F.A. Davis Co., 1973.

5 THE GENERATIONS

Barnett, Homer G. "Personal Conflicts and Cultural Change," *Social Force*, Vol. 20, (Dec. 1941), pp. 160-171.

Derry, T., and Trevor I. Williams. *A Short History of Technology*. New York: Oxford University Press, 1961.

Goodman, W.L. *The History of Woodworking Tools*. New York: David McKay Co., Inc., 1964.

Gould, Stephen Jay. *The Panda's Thumb*. New York: W.W. Norton and Co., 1980.

King, Franklin Hiram. *Farmers of Forty Centuries*. Emmaus, PA: Rodale Press, 1973.

Oakley, Kenneth P. *Man the Tool Maker*, 3rd ed. Chicago, IL: University of Chicago Press, 1964.

Sagan, Carl. *The Dragons of Eden*. New York: Random House, 1977.

Soulard, Robert. *A History of the Machine*. New York: Hawthorn Books, Inc., 1963.

Usher, A.P. *A History of Mechanical Inventions*. Cambridge: Harvard University Press, 1954.

6 THE ECOPHENOTYPIC EFFECT

Ballentyne, D. and D.R. Lovell. *A Dictionary of Named Effects and Laws in Chemistry, Physics, and Mathematics*. London: Chapman & Hall, 1920.

Ferebee, Ann. *A History of Design From the Victorian Era to the Present*. New York: Van Nostrand Reinhold Co., 1970.

Reynolds, John. *Windmills and Watermills*. New York: Praeger, 1970.

Rudofski, Bernard. *Architecture Without Architects*. New York: Doubleday, 1964.

Spicer, E.H. *Human Problems in Technological Change*. New York: Russell Sage Foundation, 1952.

7 TELEOLOGY

Bager, Bertel. *Nature as Designer*, trans. Albert Read. New York: Van Nostrand Reinhold Co., 1966.

Bates, Marston. *The Forest and the Sea, the Economy of Nature and Man*. New York: Vintage Books, 1960.

Feininger, A. *Anatomy of Nature*. New York: Crown, 1956.

Honda, Hisao, and Jack B. Fisher. "Tree Branch Angle: Maximizing Effective Leaf Area," *Science Magazine* (24 February 1978), Vol. 199, pp. 888-890.

Huntley, H.E. *The Divine Proportion*. New York: Dover Publications, 1970.

Jenny, Hans. *Cymatics*. Basel: Basilius Presse, 1967.

McMahon, Thomas. "The Mechanical Design of Trees," *Scientific American*, (July 1975), Vol. 233, No. 1, pp. 92.

Noble, J. *Purposive Evolution*. New York: Henry Holt Co., 1926.

Ritchie, J. *Design in Nature*. New York: Scribners, 1937.

Schneer, C.J. *Search For Order*. New York: Harper, 1960.

Schwenk, Theodor. *Sensitive Chaos*. London: Rudolf Steiner Press, 1965.

Sinnott, Edmund W. *The Problems of Organic Form*. New Haven, Conn.: Yale University Press, 1963.

Stevens, Peters. *Patterns in Nature*. Boston: Little Brown and Co., 1947.

Strache, W. *Forms and Patterns in Nature*. New York: Pantheon, 1956.

Weizsacker, C.F. *The History of Nature*. Chicago: Phoenix, 1949.

Weyl, Hermann. *Symmetry*. Princeton: Princeton University Press, 1952.

8 CHANCE AND THE IRRATIONAL

Baum, Robert J. *Philosophy and Mathematics*. San Francisco: Freeman, Cooper and Co.,

King, Amy, and Cecil Read. *Pathways to Probability*. New York: Holt, Reinhart and Winston, 1965.

Mandelbrot, Benoit B. *Fractals, Form, Chance, and Dimension*. San Francisco: W.H. Freeman and Co., 1977.

Spaulding, Gleasson. *A World of Chance*. New York: MacMillan and Co.

Young, Norwood. *Fortuna, Chance and Design*. New York: E.P. Dutton and Co., 1928.

Schopf, Thomas M. (ed.). *Models in Paleobiology*. San Francisco: Freeman, Cooper, and Co., 1972.

MULTIPLE CHAPTERS

Beebe, C.W. *The Bird, Its Form and Function*. New York: Henry Holt and Co., 1906. (2, 7)

Borrego, John. *Space Grids Structures*. Cambridge, Mass: The M.I.T. Press, 1968. (2, 7)

Boys, C.V. *Soap Bubbles*. New York: Dover Pub., Inc., 1959. (2, 7)

Critchlow, Keith. *Order in Space*. New York: The Viking Press, 1969. (2, 7)

Giedion, Siegfried. *Mechanization Takes Command*. New York: Oxford University Press, 1948. (4, 5, 6)

Herkimer, Herbert. *The Engineers Illustrated Thesaurus*. New York: Chemical Pub., Co., 1980.

Hertel, Heinrich. *Structure, Form, Movement*. New York: Reinhold Publishing Corporation, 1966. (2, 7)

Klem, N. *A History of Western Technology*. New York: Charles Scribners, 1959. (4, 5, 6)

Leakey, Richard E., and Rodger Lewin *Origins*. New York: E.P. Dutton, 1978. (4, 5)

McHale, John. *R. Buckminster Fuller*. New York: George Braziller, 1962. (2, 7)

McKim, Robert. *Experiences in Visual Thinking.*, (2nd Edition). Monterey, California: Brooks/Cole Pub. Co., 1980. (4, 5)

McLoughlin, John C. *Synapsida*. New York: The Viking Press, 1980. (2, 7)

Mumford, Lewis. *Technics and Civilization*. New York: Harcourt, Brace, 1934. (4, 5, 6)

Mumford, Lewis. *The Pentagon of Power*. New York: Harcourt, Brace, Jovanovich Inc., 1970. (4, 5)

Mumford, Lewis. *Art and Technics*. New York: Columbia University Press, 1952. (4, 5, 6)

Phillips, F.C. *An Introduction to Crystallography*, (3rd Edition). Glasgow: The University of Glasgow Press, 1963. (7, 2)

Sloane, Eric. *A Museum of Early American Tools*. New York: Wilfred Funk Inc., 1963. (5, 6)

Storer, Tracy, Robert Stebbins, Robert Usinger, and James Nybakken. *General Zoology*, (5th Edition), New York: McGraw Hill Book Co., 1957. (5, 7)

Usher, Abbot Payson. *A History of Mechanical Inventions*. Cambridge: Harvard University Press, 1954. (5, 6)

Williams, Christopher. *Craftsmen of Necessity*. New York: Random House Pub. Inc., 1974. (4, 5)

Wilson, Mitchell. *American Science and Invention*. New York: Simon and Schuster, 1954. (4, 5)

Wilson, Mitchell. *American Science and Invention, A Pictorial History*. New York: Simon and Schuster, 1954. (5, 6)

Wolf, Abraham. *A History of Science, Technology, and Philosophy*, (2 Vols.). New York: MacMillian Inc., 1932. (5, 6)

Wood, Donald G. *Space Enclosures Systems, The Variables of Packing Cell Design*. Bulletin 205, Columbus, Ohio: Engineering Experiment Station, Ohio State. (2, 7)

GENERAL

Alexander, Christopher. *Notes on the Synthesis of Form*. Cambridge: Harvard University Press, 1964.

Banham, Reyner. *Theory and Design in the First Machine Age*. New York: Praeger, 1960.

Carrington, Noel. *Design and Changing Civilization*, 2nd Ed. London: John Lane the Bodley Head Ltd., 1935.

Carrington, Noel. *The Shape of Things*. London: William Clowes and Sons Ltd., 1939.

Collier, Graham. *Form, Space, and Vision*. New York: Prentice Hall, 1963.

Fry, Roger. *Vision and Design*. New York: Coward-McCann, 1940.

Fuller, R. Buckminster. *Synergetics*. New York: MacMillan Pub. Co., 1975.

Giedion, Siegfried. *Space, Time, and Architecture*. Boston: Harvard University Press, 1949.

Kepes, Gyorgy. *Language of Vision*. Chicago: Paul Theobald, 1949.

Kepes, Gyorgy. *The New Landscape*. Chicago: Paul Theobald, 1956.

Lethaby, William R. *Architecture, Nature and Magic*. New York: George Braziller, 1956.

Lethaby, William R. *Form in Civilization*. London: Oxford University Press, 1957.

McHarg, Ian. *Design With Nature*. Garden City, N.Y.: Published for the American Museum of Natural History, National History Press, 1969.

Portola Institute Inc. *Whole Earth Catalogue*. Menlo Park, California: Random House, New York; Distributor, 1971.

Schmidt, George, and Robert Schenck *Form In Art and Nature*. Bassel: Basilius Presse, 1960.

Singer, Charles, (ed.), E.J. Holmyard, and A.R. Hall. *A History of Technology*, 5 Vols. London: Oxford University Press, 1956.

Thompson, Sir D'Arcy Wentworth. *On Growth and Form*, 2 Vols. Cambridge: Cambridge University Press, 1959.

Waddington, C.H., (ed.). *Towards A Theoretical Biology*, (Vol. 2). Edinburgh: Edinburgh University Press, 1969.

Wedd, Dunkin. *Pattern and Texture*. New York: Studio Books, Ltd., 1956.

Whyte, Lancelot Law. *Accent on Form*. New York: Harper, 1954.

Whyte, Lancelot Law. *Aspects of Form*. London: Lund Humphries, Ltd., 1951.

Wingler, Hans. *The Bauhaus*. ed. Joseph Stein, trans. Wolfgang Jubs and Basil Gilbert. Cambridge, Mass.: The M.I.T. Press, 1969.

Zwicky, Fritz. *Discovery, Invention, Research Through the Morphological Approach*. New York: MacMillan, 1969.

INDEX